I dedicate 'Seeking the Scots'
to three particular Scots

Francis Cecil McNab McIlwrick
& Elizabeth Dina Robertson
my parents-in-law

and Frances Elizabeth Robertson Robinson
my wife

A.R.B.R., 2006

ILLUSTRATIONS

Photographs not acknowledged above are by Betty & Arthur Robinson

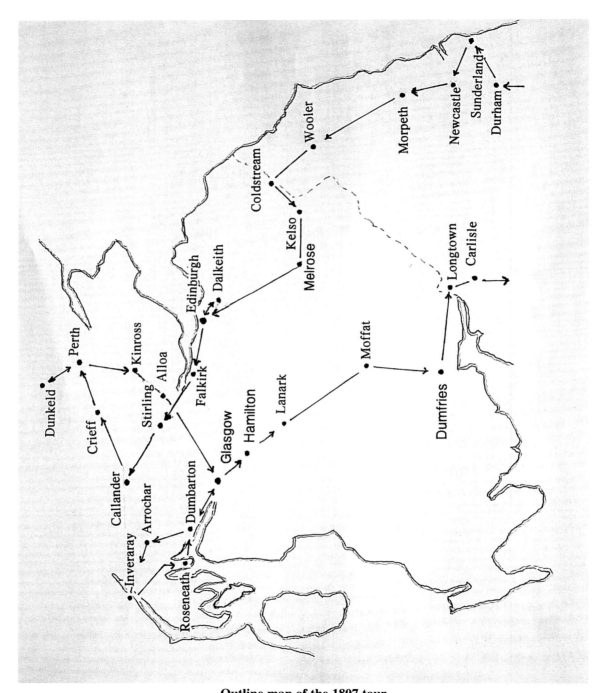

Outline map of the 1807 tour
(distance travelled in Scotland, 550 miles)

INTRODUCTION

On 10th May 1807 my great great great grandmother, aged fifty four, left Yorkshire for an eight week tour in Scotland, and recorded it in a notebook which she dedicated to her sixteen year old daughter. The notebook is headed 'Observations in Scotland in the Summer of 1807'.

She was Mrs Philothea* Perronet Thompson, wife of Thomas Thompson, a merchant and banker in Hull. His firm had been founded by the family of William Wilberforce, and the Thompsons lived in the winter months on the firm's premises at 25 High Street, Hull, now a museum of the anti-slavery movement. In summer they preferred the healthier village of Cottingham, outside Hull, where they rented houses and later built their own.

There were four children. Thomas, 24 in May 1807, was with the 95th Regiment in South America. John, 22, was a trainee lawyer in York, and travelled to Scotland with his mother. Charles, 19, was a student at Cambridge. Philothea*, 16, lived with her parents.

Mr & Mrs Thompson were staunch members of the Methodist wing of the Church of England, as John Wesley had been. Mrs Thompson's father had been one of Wesley's 'book stewards', distributing his numerous publications throughout England, and Wesley wrote her stirring letters of advice when she was a teenager[1], and may have introduced her to Thomas Thompson, who had been a Methodist preacher since his youth.

Why did Mrs Thompson and John, who were perhaps accompanied by John's aunt[2], undertake an eight hundred mile journey which took in at least forty places, north to Dunkeld and west to Inveraray? The diary does not give a reason. It was an era when 'respectable strangers' - people deemed suitable to be admitted - visited stately homes to view their treasures. Mrs Thompson visited the mansions of Dalkeith, Inveraray and Hamilton in Scotland; but that hardly justified a two month journey. Scotland itself, however, was becoming a popular destination. Thomas Pennant's two 'Tours' in Scotland, the first in 1769, gave an excellent introduction. Scott's 'Minstrelsy of the Scottish Borders' (1803) had caught the English fancy: Mrs Thompson quoted his 'Lay of the Last Minstrel' at Melrose, and 'Marmion' and the 'Lady of the Lake' came out soon after her return home. Like others of her time she sought out 'Highland' ways, 'Highland' dress and 'Highland' customs on her travels. That was another reason to cross the Border. Dorothy Wordsworth had followed a similar route to Mrs Thompson's in 1803, although her 'Recollections' would not be published for many

---

*The second syllable of the name 'Philothea' is emphasised, and pronounced "oh".

years. James Hall, a clergyman, published his 'Travels in Scotland' in 1807, subtitled 'With characters & anecdotes, and views of striking objects'. Many people were looking for the quaint or unusual in Scotland

This diary opens with a quotation from Dr Johnson, whose Scottish journal of 1775 had an enormous readership. I hope that readers of Mrs Thompson will enjoy her woman's viewpoint. It lists the materials of fine ladies' dresses in Edinburgh, while also observing the poorest. It notes "There is a large proportion of fine, tall, well-shaped and strikingly handsome persons here, especially among the Men". Often it makes remarks like "I seldom if ever saw a clean window while I was in Scotland".

Two or three months before this tour the British Parliament abolished the slave trade, after years of effort by Wilberforce and others. At the general election held soon afterwards Wilberforce was re-elected as MP for Yorkshire, with the active support of Mrs Thompson's husband; and at the same time her husband was nominated by Wilberforce's cousin, Lord Carrington, as MP for Midhurst in Sussex. Midhurst was one of the old boroughs which required no election: nomination by the patron was enough. Thompson was put into Parliament as a business man with financial talents, wide interests and Christian principles, all of which he used at Westminster for the next eleven years. So perhaps another feature of Mrs Thompson's diary - its descriptions of Scottish institutions and industries - was for her husband's information as a new MP.

The diary is dedicated to "my Philothea's amusement and pleasure". The Thompsons' daughter was born in 1791. An active-minded girl, in an age when brothers had far more opportunities, I have a letter written by her at the age of eleven, listing the unusual things in the "Museum" she kept. In 1809 her mother wrote that she wanted Philothea to "improve time and opportunity"; and we know that the teenager studied the classics, modern languages, music, painting and literature, probably at home. In the background was the tuberculosis which attacked her and her mother, took them into painful medical treatment, and killed them both in 1823.

**Mrs. P.P. Thompson:
a silhouette portrait**

Thomas Thompson MP, husband of the diarist

Post-chaise travel

Travel by road in 1807 was undoubtedly tiring, but increasingly possible. Roads were improving now that Telford and McAdam had shown that a well-drained highway could be level, without its former dangerous camber; and that when a top layer of small stones was added it was made firm by hooves and carriage wheels[3].

It is impossible to say how much of Mrs Thompson's roads had been 'improved' in these ways. I am sure that many miles were a hard slog. She makes little comment upon them, except to pronounce some sections "dreary", by which I think she means 'very tiring' - or 'very wet'. Her diary only once describes the weather, on a day when "every carriage and horseman was splashed to the middle" on a road "sloppy from constant rain". A two-month tour must have included all conditions, as I was reminded when I went to photograph the idyllic scene of her Loch Lomond crossing and found it under a downpour, with Ben Lomond lost in cloud.

The only references to Mrs Thompson's vehicles indicate that they were post-chaises. These were carriages hired from their owners, who were often inn keepers, to travel an agreed distance before horses, vehicle, or both, were changed. They were pulled by one, two or four horses, and took from one to three, occasionally four, passengers, who occupied a seat facing forward. The driver or 'post-boy' (who could be a man of any age) rode postilion on one of the horses. This allowed a window in the front of the chaise which a coach, with its driver on the front, did not[4].

C. Gray, writing a year after Mrs Thompson's journey, compared 'post-chaising' with travel by mail coach. The mail was the fastest form of stage coach - and the most expensive, since it carried few passengers. Chaises provided privacy, said Gray, but were more likely to be robbed. A chaise cost about 1 shilling a mile, which was expensive for a passenger travelling alone, but for three passengers sharing at 4 pence each it was a similar cost to the mail coach. He advised passengers against the common practice of paying their chaise driver extra to drive faster or better: that simply made drivers more "mercenary and insolent".

Horses and men were dying in thousands in the Napoleonic wars at that time, but Gray shows commendable sympathy for the post-chaise horses of Britain. "A post-chaise and pair will go 7 or 8 miles an hour 'with ease', as we phrase it. How the poor animals would phrase it, could they give their opinion, is another matter." The mail coach horse, travelling at similar average speed, pulled a great load but was changed every 12 miles, and then rested until its next scheduled journey. The post-horse might finish a stage and straight away be hired again, travelling up to 50 miles a day in all, and often carrying a post-boy on its back as well as pulling the chaise. "The life of a post-horse is a most pitiable one"[5].

I hope that Mrs Thompson's party were considerate to the horses which pulled them through Scotland. An average day's journey for them seems to have been 20-25 miles (York to Thirsk, for example; Edinburgh to Falkirk; or Dunkeld to Kinross).

Two-horse and four-horse chaises
by W. H. Pyne (1808)

Notes on the style of the diary

I have copied the diary as Mrs Thompson wrote it. Thus the reader will find the words 'though' and 'through' written 'tho' and 'thro'. She generally showed nationality with a small letter: 'english', 'scotch', 'erse'. I have retained her spellings, and only where they seem improbable, have I added '[sic]'. She used very few apostrophes, as the text shows, but she used very many commas, and I have reduced those for easier reading.

This diary was not written every day: it was partly compiled from "memorandums". One entry in Edinburgh states "I forget whether this was in Edinburgh or Glasgow"; though the writer had not yet reached Glasgow. At a Dumbarton glassworks, as she records men's hours of work, she adds "So say my memorandums, which I believe are accurate, although ...". At the Loch Lomond inn, "I might have made many remarks if I had been within reach of writing materials; but now they have escaped me". Even the heartfelt description of how "the state of the weather and the state of the Traveller" influences what is written, which appears at the beginning of the diary, may have been written later, as a comment on the whole Scottish experience.

Acknowledgements

I am very grateful to my cousin Nigel Hughes, who owns our mutual ancestor's 1807 diary, for his ready agreement to its publication. In 2005 I found that a further copy, also in her handwriting, exists at the Brotherton Library, Leeds University (MSS 277/4/22); but Nigel Hughes' is the one I have used.

Thanks too to my cousin Martin Thompson for providing Mrs Thompson's silhouette portrait, her only known likeness; and to each of the individuals and institutions who have so kindly allowed me to print the illustrations listed. They are named in the List of Illustrations.

I am grateful to Karen Hyman of York for putting my much-altered typescript into a proper state for printing; and to Maurice McIlwrick of Edinburgh for the friendship and skill he displayed in putting such a range of illustrations onto disk.

My wife Betty has encouraged me in what has proved a lengthy project, and a number of her good suggestions are incorporated here. Literally and metaphorically, we have followed much of Mrs Thompson's journey together.

The Notes at the back of the book show my sources. Some are books listed in the Bibliography. Some are Scottish Libraries, who have given prompt and efficient help. Some are individual Scots, men and women, who generously took time and trouble to answer my letters of enquiry. They too appear in the Notes, e.g. "John Brown (Glasgow): information supplied."

OBSERVATIONS IN SCOTLAND
IN THE SUMMER OF 1807

OBSERVATIONS IN SCOTLAND
IN THE SUMMER OF 1807

"Ignorance and astonishment are reciprocal, and I am conscious that mine are the observations of one who has seen but little." (Dr Johnson)

This little sketch of our Northern tour is dedicated to my Philothea's amusement and information. I shall therefore indulge in reflections, or confine myself to bare recital, as inclination may dictate.

The diary opens with a quotation from Dr Johnson's epic "Journey to the Western Islands of Scotland", published in 1775. Only the ignorant are astonished by new experiences, said Johnson; and those who see more have greater understanding.

North to the Border
10-15 May 1807

We set out from York 10 May; dined at Thirsk, the Church of which Town is a venerable Gothic structure, very capacious, and has a grammar school adjoining. The churchyard pleasant with a stream of water and a wooden bridge on the side, and comfortable Inn like an old respectable Mansion house.

The next day we dined at Darlington. We thought the country fine between this and Durham, but the roads were rugged and heavy with the quantity of rain. Here let me remark how much the state of the weather, as well as the state of the Traveller, influences descriptions of this sort. A prospect which will in a fine day appear delightful will in a gloomy season frequently lose all its charms; and when a traveller is exhausted with fatigue, the garden of Eden itself might excite but languid admiration; whereas when he begins his journey on a fine morning, in full vigour of body and mind, a very moderate scenery may seem enchanting.

> *Other travellers might describe the beauty of nature and the wildness of waterfalls. Mrs Thompson occasionally did so, but realised how much her vision was affected by the weather, the roads, or just by being tired.*

Durham is a place of singular appearance, with few good houses, and the Streets narrow and irregular. It must always be a dirty place from the nature of the soil, but it was now particularly dirty from the wetness of the season. The Bishops Castle, and the cathedral, are venerable, and there are fine slopes and walks round the city. The Episcopal palace contains large airy rooms, but no pictures, and the furniture has neither sufficient antiquity or elegance to recommend it. There were, however, two curious inlaid Tables, one of brass and Tortoise shell, the other of ebony and mother of pearl. The prospect from the palace windows is good, and there is a fine Terrace, and winding shady walk between the river and the Palace wall.

> *Durham Castle was one of the palaces of the Bishops of Durham until 1832, when Durham University was founded in and around it.*

The Cathedral is very magnificent. The chief part was built in 1083, but the part called our Ladys chapel is said to have been built in the seventh century. The Pulpit is finely inlaid with figures of the apostles. The clock was made in 1632, and shews the day of the month and age of the moon as well as the hour of the day.

The Norman part of the Cathedral was not built "in 1083", but in forty years from 1093. "Our Lady's chapel", now called the Galilee, is later, but the tomb of Bede is there, and he died at the close of the 7th century. The clock is of Scottish significance. Its carving includes a thistle, and it is said to have been spared by Scots prisoners confined in the Cathedral in 1650, when they burned other woodwork to keep themselves warm.

Part of the [Cathedral] building was under repair, and large portions of cement were forming to repair the battlements. Several statues nearly as large as life were formed of the same cement in imitation of the antique, and to replace the mouldering figures of saints and sovereigns that ornamented the roof. Many sacred vestments of gold and of singular beauty were shown to us, curiously wrought in figures representing the Crucifixion and other scriptural histories. These are said to be 500 years old. Cromwells soldiers cut off the heads of many statues on Tombs in the nave. We saw 'venerable Bedes' tomb in the Lady's chapel, the simplicity of which preserved it from violence.

What is called the College is an open kind of square, entered by a large Gate-way, and having houses on two sides which are occupied by the Prebendaries. From a high terrace in the garden of our Inn we overlooked the whole city, which stands on the side of a Hill; and the tops of a considerable number of the houses appeared beneath our feet.

The "cement" work was very recent. In 1806 the architect William Atkinson had advised the Dean & Chapter that worn stonework on the huge central tower should no longer be chiselled away, but coated with 'Parker's' (or 'Roman') Cement. This very hard substance, he said (and he had a financial interest in promoting it), would match the mossy appearance of the tower, and would express Edmund Burke's idea of 'sublimity'. It could also replace worn statues. Mrs Thompson describes the work in 1807. In 1808 there was criticism of the results; work was suspended; and ultimately all the cement was removed.[1]

The road to Sunderland was uncommonly hilly, and the country round about appeared barren. We hastened to see the Iron bridge, which is indeed a most stupendous work. Light and beautiful on the top, and wonderfully curious in the construction, as we saw below, having descended 117 stone stairs. The Town is uncommonly handsome; the streets spacious, and regularly intersecting each other, and remarkably well-paved: notwithstanding which we were astonished at the number of Pattens we everywhere met with. It was old May-day, and probably a Fair was held there; for the concourse was very great, and probably the morning might have been unfavourable, which might account for the general use of Pattens.

The "stupendous work", still in use as Wearmouth Bridge, was only the second iron bridge to be constructed when it opened in 1796. Its arch, with cast iron ribs, soared above the ships which passed beneath[2]. Old May-day was twelve days after 1st May, on the same basis that old Christmas Day was twelve days after 25th December. Pattens were iron frames fastened under the shoes to lift them above the mud.

An early print of Wearmouth Bridge, Sunderland

The country round Sunderland is very pleasant, but the road to Newcastle is hilly and rough. The town [Newcastle] is very large, and might have appeared handsome if it had been seen before Sunderland. The streets are wide, and the houses moderately good, and the whole more regular than the generality of old Towns. The Orphan House is an uncouth building in which much room is lost, and convenience little consulted, yet it is venerable and interesting from its original design, and the number of pious persons who for a succession of years have occupied it. We called on Mrs A.D., one of the excellent of the earth. A Methodist of the old School, pious, friendly and unassuming; aiming at a heavenly life in a mortal body.

Mrs A.D. is the first of various women whom Mrs Thompson called on during her journey, as she was accustomed to do at home. When she uses the word "pious", in this journal and in her letters, it is always a compliment, denoting a strong and simple faith.

The election at Morpeth engaged every chaise, and left us sufficient time to wander about Newcastle; which is not very well paved, but has the convenience of broad stone crossings in different directions. There are four Churches and a chapel of ease in Newcastle. The principal Church is that of St Nicholas. It is uncommonly large, and commodiously fitted up with large wainscot pews, and long seats in the middle of the aisles. There are some fine monuments, particularly one of Dorothy Wise. There are daily prayers at St Nicholas.

Visitors to St Nicholas Church, early 19th century

St Nicholas' Church is now Newcastle Cathedral. "Wainscot" pews may be box pews, as compared with the "long seats". The people in the illustration are being shown a Maddison family monument: Dorothy Wise's cannot now be traced[3].

Parliamentary elections were held over a period of one or two weeks, to allow electors to travel from a distance. While this one went on at Morpeth, Mrs Thompson's husband was giving his support to William Wilberforce, who was standing at York.

We found the charges at Newcastle beyond what we had hitherto met with. The lowest order of people appeared uncommonly squalid; and the language was not always very intelligible. The surrounding countryside is flat: the roads, a mixture of coal and clay, and very sloppy from constant rain. Every carriage and horseman was splashed to the middle. There were several fine seats near the road, of which we saw little more than the entrances. Sir M W Ridley's had a pillar with a large Ox on it on each side of his gateway.

Road maps of the period often identified gentlemen's estates. Sir M.W. Ridley's entrance, designed by the architect James Wyatt[4], is on the old road close to today's A1.

Sir M.W. Ridley's gateway with "oxen"

16 May we spent at Morpeth, a neat, handsome country town. The Church is at a considerable distance. A Tower for the bells is erected in the middle. The Jail is in the public street, and prisoners are seen in the grated windows; one with a child, another with a flute; probably Debtors.

St Mary's church is south of the town, on the old Great North Road; and there is a clock tower in the town centre, though it is not part of the church.

We intended to have slept at Whittingham, having travelled "over the mountain and over the moor" till after sun-set. But the Inn [at Whittingham] was full of soldiers, and we were obliged to set forward to Wooler-Cottage, where we arrived at near Midnight, after traversing a very lonely road where we scarcely saw a house or a living creature [though it was] not so rugged as the former stage [to Whittingham]. The Moon gave a feeble light, and a gloomy stillness prevailed around us, which the Driver sometimes interrupted to point to memorials of other times, which we could not see, and told a story of a murdered man who had been concealed in the bank we had just crossed, which, with the attendant circumstances of solitude and gloom, almost petrified us with horror.

A frightening journey indeed. The route from Morpeth to the Scottish border at Coldstream was similar to today's A697. In 1807 carriages took the Wooler & Breamish turnpike road as far as Wooler. The first part of the turnpike linked villages on or near the A697, but a mile north of Longframlington it headed directly and dramatically across Rimside Moor to Whittingham. That part ("the most daunting stretch of road since London"[5]) can still be followed on foot. The murder story which the driver told Mrs Thompson was one of many tales of the Moor.

We reached at last a very comfortable Inn [at Wooler-Cottage], where a good fire and every necessary refreshment banished the recollection of past inconveniences.

The next morning all around us looked extremely pleasant. A large Garden, rather tastefully laid out, with everything for use or moderate beauty. Sheep in the adjacent fields, the whole neither so high or so barren as some we had lately crossed. The country seemed improving on us, and there was no comparison between the fertility of the entrance into Scotland thus far and the country for twenty miles behind us.

The Tankerville Arms, former Wooler Cottage inn

Wooler Cottage refers to the still flourishing Tankerville Arms Hotel in Wooler. This old coaching inn was once called the "cottage" because it accommodated guests to Chillingham Castle, seat of Lord Tankerville[6]. An 1827 local directory shows that the 'Wellington' coach from Edinburgh to London called there, as did the horse-drawn waggons which had replaced packhorses not long before[7].

The barren ranges of hills which rose in succession for many miles in Northumberland   - where a few scattered spots seemed forced into a degree of fruitfulness, in spite of natural sterility - have given place to a lively verdant country with a beautiful variety of hill and dale. The pastures are tolerably rich, and besprinkled with habitations of various orders, many of which were properly huts, and seemed hardly designed for human residence, but others were remarkable for their neatness, and seemed strong enough to defy wind and weather for a century to come. Here and there a venerable antique or a handsome modern edifice enlivened the scene. The view round Mill-field was very fine.

The writer had left the "barren ranges" of the Cheviots, and the country was softer now. The Millfield Plain, which was a lake after the Ice Age retreated from the hills, is rich agricultural land.

The Gullery at New Pallins-burn was uncommonly curious. For about a square mile the ground, which was slightly overflowed with water, was covered by perhaps thousands of Sea-gulls sitting on their nests wherever the Land or rushes were above the water, and flying around in every direction, making a confused noise like the sound of a hundred grindstones.

The house shown as Pallinsburn on today's maps was New Pallinsburn then, rebuilt not long before 1807. In front of the house and adjacent to the A697 (but hidden today by trees) is the large, shallow lake which Mrs Thompson called the "Gullery". It remained a nesting-place for black-headed gulls until recent times. Many breeds of duck have taken their place[8].

At this point Mrs Thompson was within a mile or two of the battlefield of Flodden, where the Scots army of James IV was defeated by the English in 1513. She did not visit it, but no doubt read Walter Scott's poem about it, 'Marmion', when it came out in 1808.

The Tweed rolled majestically by our side for many miles; and a handsome stone bridge took us over it near Coldstream. Here we first saw the practice of walking without shoes or stockings. Many decent females were without the latter; and to our surprise the custom appears hitherto to be confined to females.

Six days after leaving York our party crosses the Tweed and arrives in Scotland, with less fuss than many modern tourists who have come from York in four hours. The "handsome bridge" was designed by Smeaton, and opened in 1766. Mrs Thompson probably wrote this part of her diary in retrospect: the Tweed did not roll by her side on the way to Coldstream, but as she travelled on from Coldstream to Kelso.

**The "handsome bridge" at Coldstream,
with Scotland on the further shore**

Chapel, Kirk and Abbey
16-18 May

Saturday 16 of May we took up our rest at Kelso, with a view to the proper employment of the Sabbath. All the congregations in Scotland, episcopal, Presbyterian or Methodists, begin their services on the Sunday at eleven o'clock in the forenoon, and two in the afternoon. We attended on Sunday 17 May at the episcopal chapel in the morning; a neat modern building, with a sweet-toned Organ which was played in a manner more suited to religious worship than many that are heard south of the Tweed. The Congregation gathered very slowly, and not more than about a hundred attended in all. The Minister wore his Gown thro the whole service, and read distinctly, with little of the Scottish accent. The Clerk read still better. The Sermon was decent, tho not evangelical, and was preparatory to the Sacrament, which was to be administered a fortnight after. The Congregation was not remarkable either for attention or carelessness. The clerk at the chapel was remarkably civil, and very inquisitive to know who we were, and whether we were English!

In Scotland, the Episcopal church (governed by bishops) had a difficult time in the 18th century. The Church of Scotland by law was Presbyterian, and Episcopalian congregations were usually only permitted where their priest had been appointed in England. Kelso's "Episcopal chapel" was built in 1769 on this basis, and, as regulation eased, was recognised by law by the time Mrs Thompson attended it.[1]

The Episcopal chapel stands in a small enclosure like a Garden, with some large Tombs at the upper end for "Douglas" and high people, and the poor occupied some almost imperceptible graves near the entrance.

A surviving gravestone today records the death of Harriot Bristow, aged one week, two months before Mrs Thompson's visit; of Harriot's father in that year; and of her mother almost fifty years later.

After service, we walked by the Tweed side. The surrounding view was delightful. Whoever describes Scotland as the seat of sterility and wretchedness must go thro it with closed eyes. Kelso is certainly at least equal to most Towns of the same size and importance in England, both for buildings and scenery. A handsome stone bridge of five arches crosses the river. Several fine houses are in view, and the country round is verdant, and many fine Groves are interspersed. One of the most interesting objects in the Town is the Abbey; a fine old ruin, enough of which remains to show that it has been very magnificent, and to contain the bells which serve to give notice for assembling both in the english Chapel and the Kirk. The Porch, which was wont to admit the Warrior or

Religious of other times, now contained only the Fire engine.

The five arched bridge was very new, built by Rennie in 1803 to replace one destroyed by floods in 1797. From there the view includes the finest of the "fine houses", Floors Castle. It may seem strange that the bells of an Abbey built in a very different religious era should summon worshippers to a reformed Kirk. In fact the Abbey, even when it was a monastic church, had also housed a parish church; and it served the town under 'reformed' clergy until the Kirk shown below was built.[2]

We had little time for dinner and hastened to the Kirk, which was a large octagon, with Pews so arranged as to suit the form of the building, and a small Table in each pew, answerable to its shape. The side pews were oblong and their Tables likewise. A large pew in the centre was an octagon with a Table of the same form. Such of the pews as were made with divers corners, to fill up cavities, had a Table in some sort of agreement. All of which, from the Gallery where we sat, had a very odd appearance.

The Kirk, designed by Nisbet, had opened in 1773, when services ceased to be held in the Abbey. The octagonal shape was a very unusual one; though it was a shape advocated by John Wesley, who visited this building in 1790.

The interior of Kelso Old Kirk (19th century photograph)

The Minister was a respectable middle aged man, without anything very distinguishing about him except his band. He was dressed in handsome black clothes, and black gloves which he wore the whole time, with his hands clasped together and hanging down before him. Of course, he had no action. His voice was clear and distinct, without anything of the drawl or whine we had expected, and he gave from 'Consider the lilies of the field', an ingenious and florid descant on the course of vegetation and the beauties of Spring, etc. But excepting some Moral reflections on the uncertainty of life, and some slight reference to the resurrection, there was no trait of the doctrines of the Gospel, except that his doxologies were explicitly orthodox. The Congregation was more numerous and more shewy than that in the Morning, but by no means more serious. They stood in prayer time, and many were looking around the whole time. The singing was very dismal; and the service not longer than that at the episcopal chapel. The building was handsome, but not clean. A large open space served as a burial place to the Kirk.

Ministers of the Scottish Kirk had a reputation for declaiming in a certain way, with a "drawl or whine". Black gloves were frequently worn by ministers until the early 1900s. "He had no action" suggests that he used no gestures[3]. Much more important to the writer, however, was that the minister used his text - 'Consider the lilies of the field', Matthew 6.28 - for a mere "descant on nature" instead of a "Gospel doctrine" of the providence of God.

Our Inn was in a large open space called the Horse Market. The children were playing there in little groups on the Saturday, and grown people were employed, or walking in different directions, yet without the clamour usually found in places of the same sort in England. But on Sunday morning scarcely a creature was to be seen. No children were playing, or persons walking in the Street. In the latter part of the day many people collected in little companies, but with a considerable degree of decorum.

Their inn was probably the Cross Keys, which is still in the square adjacent to the Horse Market. In 1807 it was owned by George and Mary Yule, who ran coaches from the Cross Keys to Edinburgh three times a week, the 45 mile journey taking 10 hours in summer and 12 in winter. "In winter, the outside passengers sometimes froze into position and had to be helped down from their seats"[4].

We searched in vain for a Methodist chapel in the evening. No such place seemed to be known in Kelso, tho we learned afterwards that a few Methodists reside there and meet the preachers at Melrose a few times in the year; and there had been once a greater number [at Kelso], as well as a Preaching house.

The poor seemed more decent here than in many parts of Northumberland, and their behaviour was remarkably courteous and respectful, tho "I dan na ken" was the answer we received to most of our inquiries. We met with little however in proof of cleanliness. Even the genteeler women had an air of slatternliness not common in England. But the gentlemen appeared rather over dressed; Qeues [queues: the hair tied back], powder etc being more in use than they are with us. The houses in Kelso are chiefly built with a dirty looking grey stone, [although] a few modern buildings looked more white and lively. The houses in some of the villages in Scotland are built of large rough stones with the interstices filled up with mud or mortar; but the corners, and the edges of the doors and windows, were ornamented with square stones of different colours, so placed and varied as to form a border, which greatly improved the appearance.

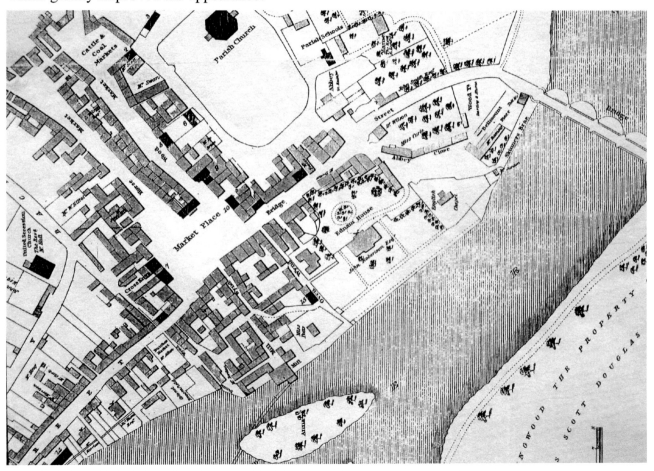

Plan of Kelso by John Wood (1823)
showing Parish Church, English Chapel and Cross Keys Inn

May 18 we proceeded to Melrose thro a pleasant country interspersed with gentlemen's seats, cottages, plantations etc, the Tweed winding thro, and the Eildon hills being in sight most of the way.

The three peaks of the Eildons which stand over Melrose, named 'Trimontium' by the Romans, have attracted travellers in every century.

The fine remains of Melrose Abbey were highly gratifying, tho perhaps hardly equal to our expectations. The eastern window was amazingly light and fine, and the carving of fruits, flowers and foliage incomparable, tho disgraced by the frequent occurrence of grotesque figures - Fidlers, Bagpipers, etc etc. A Douglas, slain at the battle of Otterbourne, with many kings and warriors, rested in the Chancel.

The ruins of Melrose Abbey, far more complete than those at Kelso, include a huge array of mediaeval carving on the outer walls. Mrs Thompson would have seen biblical figures as well as "disgraceful" fiddlers and pipers: but the last straw, for her, may have been the Abbey's carving of a bagpiping pig.

Melrose: the "amazingly fine" East end, and "grotesque figures"

A part of the Abbey now in use for public worship was very wretched, and hardly admitted of our walking upright. A large kind of Pulpit stands abroad, from which the Preacher "demonstrates" at sacramental seasons, when the Congregations are very large. An intelligent man shewed us the whole, and seemed much interested, and to share in our pleasure. He had Scott's 'Lay of the Last Minstrel' at his finger ends, and expressed his obligation to that charming writer for a great increase in visitants. We were inclined to survey "Fair Melrose by the pale moonlight" as it was just the suitable season, and our guide assured us it was still worth seeing by moonlight, tho not in the degree which Scott describes. But our Inn was un-inviting, and we left Melrose the same day, tho not without some reluctance.

> The "wretched place for worship" was in fact the parish church, which had been sited within the ruined Abbey since 1610. It stood inside the monks' choir of the Abbey church, and traces of it still remain. It had its own roof, and a gallery inside, hence Mrs Thompson's impression of "hardly walking upright"[5]. In 1810, not long after this visit, a new parish church was built.
>
> Scott wrote his 'Lay of the Last Minstrel' in 1805. Mrs Thompson had clearly read its advice to see Melrose Abbey by moonlight, which - said the poem - suited the sadness of its ruins.[6]

The contrasts of Edinburgh
19 May-1 June

18 May. We proceeded to Bank-house, and the next day arrived at Edinburgh. We took up our abode at a principal Hotel in the new Town, and found a strange mixture of shew and inconvenience. We had seventy stairs to ascend whenever we returned to our lodgings. We had no fastenings to our chamber doors, and when I remonstrated with the servant, and asked her what had been done by the people who occupied the rooms before us, she said,in the broad scottish accent, "They niver trobell'd no keys". Our rooms were crowded with furniture and abundance of pictures, but nothing was clean. The houses in the new town are handsome and in general uniform, and seldom more than three or four stories high. But in the old town they are usually six 'flats' from the bottom, and sometimes eight or ten. Some of the streets are carried over other streets; and you look thro apertures and see carriages and passengers at a great distance below. At least, this is the case in one instance.

The New Town of Edinburgh was the area of orderly Georgian streets to the north of the old city. Mrs Thompson's "hotel" and "lodgings" seem to be the same place. It is likely that they were Liddle's Lodgings in South Hanover Street, off Princes Street and opposite the Mound. John Thompson stayed there in 1809 when at Edinburgh University, and his mother wrote to him there: "I am exceedingly glad ..., that you have got to Mrs Liddel's ... I suppose you have the Room at the end, which is so crowded with pictures ... Pray remember me kindly to your Hostess". This surely indicates that Mrs Thompson was there in 1807[1].

Edinburgh fashions, 1800 (left) and 1810 (right)

The College is the outline of a noble building. The pillars are very high and large, and are said to be each made of one solid stone. One of the Inhabitants told us the College was "a monument of scotch pride and poverty", for it remains unfinished, and probably always will remain so.

Edinburgh University had about 1200 students in 1807. Its handsome 'College' building, now called the Old College, was designed by Robert Adam and William Playfair, and work began on it in 1786 - but was stopped from 1793 to 1816 for lack of funds.[2]

Before we reached Edinburgh we saw great number of females without hats or stockings, and often without shoes. Men and boys were seldom seen without them, and indeed they usually appear better dressed in Scotland than the women; and their employments are in general far less laborious. The dress of the poorer women is usually a stuff or wolsey petticoat - a short linen bedgown - a large mob strait down the face, and a coloured handkerchief twisted about the neck. Till they are married they generally wear their hair loose; and I never recollect to have seen amongst the poor what might appear to be a middle-aged woman, for as soon as they marry, or cease to be accounted girls, they assume those disguising coifs, and every vestige of youth is lost.

'Strait' - a different adjective from 'straight' - means close or narrow. Perhaps the mob cap fitted close to the head.

The proportion of children is very great, but few of them seem employed except when there are manufactories. Indeed most of the children get some degree of learning; but there is so little attention paid to the convenience or comfort of life, that when there is not any washing or rough household work to do, they generally hang about idly, or lie on the road side or in the corners of streets like Pigs. Wearing no stockings, they have no need to knit. The mode of washing is of a very rough kind. Much linnen is washed in the river; or if it is very dirty it is stamped on, with naked feet, in a Tub of water. Persons who are more exact finish it with soap in the usual way; and the linnen looks a tolerable colour, tho it is seldom perfectly clean.

In Edinburgh people appear much more dressed than those of equal rank in London. Pelisses were pretty generally worn by the Ladies, tho it was summer; many of them of the richest twilled sarsonets, and others of slighter materials, but all ornamented in various ways. Women of inferior rank wore fine stuffs, bordered and variously decorated with broad ribbons of divers colours; a rose red, for instance, on a grey Pelisse.

'Arrival of the country relatives', by Alexander Carse (1812)

Carse's picture, shown on the cover of this book, is seen here in full. The country relatives are depicted arriving at a flat in the New Town.

Show and parade appeared to be the order of the day, and everyone made the utmost appearance possible. But the poor are most wretchedly dirty and squalid. The continual sight of dirty naked feet, often tied about the heels and toes with the filthiest rags, was exceptionally disgusting; and I thought I never saw such extremes of luxury and wretchedness as in Edinburgh.

I imagine that Mrs Thompson, from her attitude to life and her religious beliefs, dressed modestly, but she was quite able to describe the dresses and materials of smarter people. She was also accustomed to helping the poor at home - her letters mention it, and her husband was Guardian of the Poor in Hull in the 1801 famine there - so she must indeed have been struck by the "wretchedness" in Edinburgh.

22 May. We visited Leith, but did not see it to advantage, nor did there appear anything very interesting in the place. Next day we went over the Botanical Garden in Edinburgh. It was remarkably neat and in good order, but owing to the backwardness of the season there was not much show. There were three or four Green-houses with very curious exotics. Particularly some Dragon-trees, eighteen or twenty feet high, the young strait stem and smooth bark, and the top a tuft of leaves like a large Mop, but small in proportion to the heigth [sic]: the whole very singular. Several fine specimens of different kinds of Palm. A fine Date Palm, but does not produce in Britain. The Mimosa or Gum Arabic Tree - very beautiful; and a species of sensitive plant, uncommonly so: the branches multiplied amazingly in pairs, and the leaves likewise grow in pairs to a very great number. An uncommonly noble Aloe, which had not yet flowered. A botany-bay lilly, curious, and unlike any british flower.

These jottings seem like notes made until the writer could check the plants in the Hull lending library, to which she belonged. Edinburgh's Botanic Garden, originally a 'Physick Garden' cultivating medical plants, by now had facilities for many other species.[3]

We proceeded to Calton Hill burying ground, where a number of inclosures were built up like kind of summer houses, for the burial of different families. David Hume's Tomb was a large round Tower, many feet high and visible from a considerable distance; indeed from nearly all parts of the City.

This "burying ground", opened in the 18th century, was better laid out than more ancient churchyards. The monument to David Hume, philosopher and historian, is of 1776. Calton Hill, a marvellous site overlooking Edinburgh, also had an Observatory and Bridewell when Mrs Thompson was there.

Edinburgh from Calton Hill, with monument to Dugald Stewart
John Thompson attended his lectures in 1809

Thence we went to the new Bridewell on the same [Calton] hill, which is an institution of great promise, from the judicious mode of building and management. It is shewn to respectable strangers, but not to the Townspeople without an order from a Magistrate to avoid improper intrusion. From a small circular room, the prisoners were distinctly seen thro different apertures in the wall: each in a separate room, excepting a few of the men whose business required them to work together. The women were spinning in solitary Cells, and appeared orderly and diligent. They seldom see each other, or any visitant. Each Cell is barred in front from top to bottom, and they were ranged in rows, one set above another, like a model I have seen of Noah's ark. The men occupied the lower apartments, and were less conspicuous. In cold weather the whole is warmed by Flues properly contrived. Every attention was paid to their health and reformation. Their bed-rooms are better than those which many servants and poor housekeepers occupy with us. Each person has a separate chamber. Blankets and sheets clean and good. The beds neatly made up, with the sheet turned over a very decent rug, ready for sleeping. A New Testament laid on each bed, but no chair or other furniture was visible. Probably a box for clothes might be under the bed. The prisoners wear a suitable uniform and attend worship in a chapel of their own twice every Sunday. Those who behave the best are taken to wash, cook and clean for the [governor's?] family. We were shewn into one or two of the cells. The women manifested a sort of quiet dejection, and did not look up; and we saw only one old woman who seemed hardened and audacious. The whole establishment appeared perfectly clean and well regulated.

English Bridewells began in the 16th century to provide work for the able-bodied poor, but became places of correction for petty offenders. By 1807 various institutions sought to reform as well as to correct, advocating solitary, supervised work and exposure to religion. The Edinburgh Bridewell, designed by Robert Adam and built in 1796, apparently shared these aims. In 1808 a separate Jail appeared on Calton Hill, replacing the Tolbooth in the Old Town.[4]

The Bridewell on Calton Hill
by T. H. Shepherd (1827)

24. We attended at the High Kirk [St Giles]; a splendid building of the gothic order, at least as to the pillars and arches, imitating groves etc. Being the time of the general Assembly of Divines in Scotland, a magnificent Throne was placed opposite to the pulpit, for the representative of the Sovereign. The whole front of the gallery on three sides of the church was covered with crimson velvet, fringed I think with gold, and large crimson velvet cushions placed at equal distances. The Lord High Commissioner Ld Napier bowed respectfully on all sides; and when he sat down the rest followed his example.

The front of the Gallery was filled with Nobles, Military officers and Divines. The Preacher appeared young and insignificant; nor was his eloquence particularly suited to such an August assembly. Yet he spoke in a clear distinct voice for about five & twenty minutes, and then gave out a Psalm, and prayed as before the sermon. After which he read over again the same text, and preached for twenty minutes longer, and then concluded with singing and prayer. The insipid dulness of the Psalmody gave an air of tediousness to the service which the prayers were not calculated to remedy. The whole however was not uninteresting, tho rather metaphysical than evangelical. My thankfulness was much increased for -

> "... the solemn form
> Of ancient words which keep devotion warm
> And guide, tho bound our wishes";

as well as for being accustomed to sing as well as pray <u>with the spirit and the understanding also</u>. The whole Court and Assembly went in solemn procession to and from Church; and on the early days of the Assembly, the Military were drawn out. The concourse of people was very great.

> *What the writer meant by "evangelical", and did not find at St Giles', were words such as John Wesley had written to her in a letter when she was twenty one: "Go on, trampling upon sin and Satan, and praising Him who has put all things under your feet".* [5]

In the afternoon we attended at the episcopal chapel - a far more elegant building than the High Kirk. Indeed it exceeded, in elegant simplicity, most places of worship I have seen. The Minister was a good speaker, and made many striking and forcible remarks. It was not strictly speaking an evangelical sermon; but it contained much that was excellent. In the Eveng. [sic] we heard a useful sermon at the Methodist chapel. The congregation was small, tho the building was respectable.

There were several episcopal chapels in Edinburgh in 1807, but only two, apparently, were "elegant": St George's in York Place in the New Town (built 1792-94), which is now a casino; and the Cowgate Chapel in the Old Town (built 1772-74), which is now St Patrick's Roman Catholic Church.[6]

All the Pews in Scotland, even in the High Kirk, are built of Fir, unpainted, and only polished by continual handling. The people stand universally during prayer time; and none, at least in the Kirk, use any form of devotion either at the beginning or conclusion; but bow, curts'y and talk as tho they were in a place of amusement. In prayer time they are looking every way and appear no way engaged in the duty: and when they judge from the tone of the Minister's voice, or from the tenor of his prayer (for I never could discover any signal) that he is about to conclude, they all turn and sit down, leaving him to finish the most solemn parts of worship alone.

25. We gained admittance with some difficulty into the General Assembly of Presbyters. We were in the Gallery, but could hear little, and the high North Country dialect of many of the speakers made much of that little, unintelligible. The Lord High Commissioner was seated on a Throne, with a high dressed Page on either hand, and several other attendants. He was writing the whole time, and appeared quite uninterested in what was passing, in which he seems never to interfere.

28 [three days later]. We went thro very rainy weather to Roslyn and Dalkeith, a few miles from Edinburgh. Much of the country appeared beautifull, tho seen to such disadvantage. The ruins of Roslyn Castle were interesting chiefly on account of their antiquity. Many "tales of other times" were told us with reference to the ruins; but nothing sufficiently important to be related. It is evident that the state of sculpture was very low at the time wh. those buildings flourished, as two different events that were meant to be recorded in stone were drawn, or rather carved, in the rudest outline of a school boy's chalk.

Rosslyn Castle was built and rebuilt by the St Clair family, once Princes of Orkney. Destroyed by accidental fire in 1447, burned again by order of Henry VIII in 1544, and sacked by Cromwell's troops in 1650, it certainly had "tales of other times"[7]. Mrs Thompson seems not to have visited the nearby Rosslyn Chapel, built in 1446 and famous for its stone carving.

Dalkeith had nothing delightfull in it except the Duke of Buccleughs grounds and Palace, which are well worth seeing. The buildings are very magnificent, and there is much fine painting and noble furniture. The rooms and staircases were covered with pictures. A large portrait of a Man in a Turkish habit who was 7 feet 10 inches high, and well proportioned, who lived some years in the service of a former Duke and died at eight & twenty years of age. Many family portraits were there. A family piece of the present possessors, in small size - pleasant, sensible looking people. A large picture of the Duchess of Monmouth & Buccleugh, who is celebrated in 'The Lay of the Last Minstrel', with two of her Sons in long periwigs, tho children. Two small pictures of [Queens?] Mary and Elizabeth when girls. A portrait of Lady Jane Grey, unlike anything we conceive of her; florid, heavy and uninteresting. A lively picture of a boy opening a pye.

The very tall man was named 'Cojanus the Lapland Giant', and his portrait is now in Finland[8]. The portrait of Lady Jane Grey cannot now be traced (though Pennant described it in 1769)[9]. The Duchess and her sons, by Kneller, can still be seen. Her husband the Duke of Monmouth, illegitimate son of Charles II, was beheaded for treason against James II, but by pleading she had no part in his offence she retained her own Buccleugh inheritance for future generations.[10]

29 May. We went into Edinburgh castle. In the armoury 22,000 stand of arms are kept ready for use. Grape-shot and shot of all sizes, with Pikes, Sabres, Muskets, Cannon and every instrument of destruction. We saw the workshop for repairing and cleaning arms; grind-stones, and every other convenience.

Barnards well is a mile or two out of Edinburgh: a fine spring with a handsome stone Temple built over it, and an elegant, but gigantic, figure of the goddess of health.

During the Napoleonic Wars Edinburgh defended itself against possible invasion. The city "became a camp", and the local militias included University professors, lawyers, and "any able-bodied man of whatever rank"[11]. No doubt the Castle armoury supplied them.

Barnard's (St Bernard's) Well had been built in 1789 over a mineral spring by the Water of Leith. It still exists, with its statue of Hygeia.[12]

St Bernard's Well, with statue of Hygeia

The Observatory [opened in 1792] is on Calton Hill, and seems well situated, and is said to be well provided with astronomical instruments; but for some reason which we did not learn, it is not now shewn to strangers.

30. We visited Herriott's and Gillespie's Hospitals. The latter was founded, by a worthy Tobacconist of that name, for old men and women, about thirty of whom are comfortably supported. Each has a neat airy chamber and a good bed, etc. A large and pleasant room with a fire-place at each end serves for diningroom-sittingroom [sic] and chapel. A handsome Committee room in which is a lively picture of the Founder, a plain respectable old Man, leaning on his staff.

> *A recent foundation, Gillespie's Hospital had opened in 1805. James Gillespie, tobacco merchant and owner of a snuff mill in Colinton, had died in 1797 leaving money for the aged, and for a school which still bears his name.[13]*

Herriott's Hospital is a large building of some antiquity, ornamented, or rather loaded, with turrets and spires at the top. A hundred & fifty boys are educated in it from seven to fourteen years of age. Thirty beds are in a Chamber; and there is a sick room, which seems to be little wanted. Two large tables in the Dining room were covered with tins of milk and large portions of white bread. The children appeared lively and orderly. All the stoves are on the Rumford Plan, and two cart loads of cinders are said to serve a month where many chaldrons of Coal would be required for fire places of a common construction. All the fire that was visible, for cooking etc for so large a family, might have been contained in a small Back stove. All the contrivances here for cooking, washing, drying etc are excellently calculated to save expence and labour.

The admirable Rumford was an American, originally named Benjamin Thompson, whose social reforms included improvements in Dublin hospitals and the invention of new devices for domestic economy. He died in 1814.[14]

The windows of the school are wired with strong wire like a Parrot's cage, and some of the lower ones are strongly grated, which gives the edifice something of the appearance of a prison. Many capital scholars proceed from this school, and many eminent men have returned their tribute of gratitude for their education and advancement. Several testimonies of this kind hang round the Committee room; and Donations have been made and legacies bequeathed to a large amount, equally to the honour of the Donor and the benefit of the Institution. When the boys leave the school, £30 is given with them as an apprentice fee, and probably they have still further advantages. If they shew great capacity, and inclination for learning, they are supported at the University. There is a handsome Chapel where the children assemble twice a day for prayer. On Sunday they attend the Kirk. On the first of June is the school festival, at which time new scholars are admitted, and those who have finished their learning leave the school. All the scholars are new clothed on that day, and a Sermon is preached at the Grey friars Kirk, at which all the charity children in Edinburgh attend.

With some difficulty, we gained admittance [to Greyfriars Kirk] on that day. But the crowd was very great, particularly in leaving the church, as the people pressed to see the children walk; and the Herriott boys [afterwards?] enter their habitation, which was curiously decorated - especially the Statue of their founder - with garlands and wreaths of flowers. Those who saw it, thought it was well worth crowding for; but I did not.

"Curiously decorated": the Heriot festival, painted in 1859

There was not much regularity observed in the Church, nor did the children sit in ranks, as is usual for charity children in England. The Girls were hardly to be seen at all. Two anthems were sung by the Children, but very indifferently. A very excellent sermon was preached on the occasion; and the Magistrates and Governors of the Schools, then the Masters, and lastly the children, were seriously and earnestly addressed.

In the Church Yard [of Greyfriars], many Charnel houses and burying places for the dead were erected round, as is usual in Scotland. Many very heavy Monuments were sunk, either by age or design, deep in the ground. Many inscriptions were effaced, and statues decapitated.

One remarkable stone, large and unornamented, was in memory of those who lost their lives in the cause of the covenant, eighteen hundred of whom were said to have died by the hands of the executioner, or otherwise slain. The rhymes are rather uncouth, and breathe a vindictive spirit. A Duke of Argyll; Guthrie; and Frazer; are particularly named. The date is about 1661.

"Uncouth and vindictive" at first sight, perhaps; but the stone records eighteen thousand (not eighteen hundred) men and women killed as Covenanters between 1661 and 1688, for - as the stone says - "witnessing to Christ their King against the lust of prelatists". The National Covenant against Charles' I's imposition of a Prayer Book on Scotland had been signed in this very kirkyard in 1638 - and in 1679 twelve hundred Covenanters, defeated at Bothwell Bridge, were imprisoned there among the "burying places" Mrs Thompson mentions.

The Covenanter stone (erected 1704, restored 1771) at Greyfriars

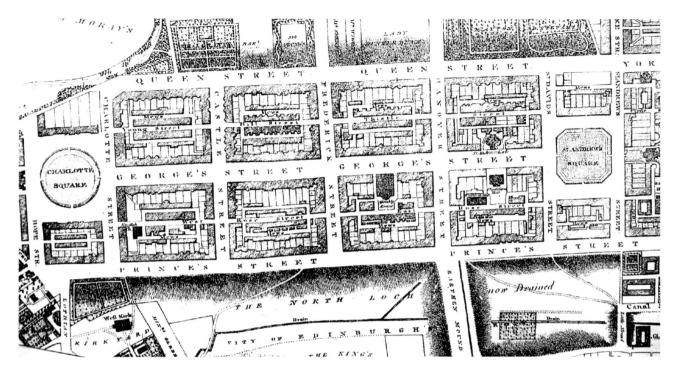

The New Town: part of Ainslie's map of Edinburgh (1804)

The diary later describes the New Town as "three principal streets from east to west, said to be one mile in length", with "two smaller parallel streets" between, and "wide streets crossing from north to south". That is exactly the area set out by James Craig in his winning entry (1766) for the design of the New Town. It obviously stood out as a complete unit in 1807, though further development northwards was going on by then.

The "principal streets from east to west" were George Street, named for George III, flanked, at a lower level, by Queen Street for his wife and by Prince's (later Princes) Street for his eldest son. The "smaller, parallel" streets between were named Thistle and Rose, after the national emblems. Squares at either end of Craig's long streets were named for St Andrew and St George (though the latter was renamed Charlotte as the city already had a George Square).[15]

The Mound, which spans the former North Loch, was made of earth dug from the foundations of the New Town. This map shows it as the 'Earthen Mound'.

Sunday 31. We attended, morning and afternoon, at St Andrew's Kirk, an elegant erection in the New Town. We did not know or much approve the morning Preacher, tho all the sermons in the Kirk are well digested and arranged, and generally well delivered. In the afternoon, a very masterly sermon was delivered by Principal Hill. It was indeed in a very superior style, tho rather more provincial in the dialect than any public speaker we had heard before; yet remarkably eloquent and forcible. A fine, clear, commanding voice, and sound doctrine as far as it went; but not calculated for much improvement to a people uncircumcised in heart and ears, as it is to be feared most of the gay auditors at St Andrew's were. Yet careless and inconsiderate as this congregation in particular appeared, Principal Hill gained their attention, while, with all the wisdom of sound speech, he preached to them Jesus and the resurrection, from Matthew chapter 22, verses 23-29.

"Uncircumcised in heart and ears" was how Stephen, the first Christian martyr, described his hearers, and they stoned him to death for it! George Hill, Principal of St Mary's College, St Andrews, had a reputation for bringing together people of varying viewpoints, and as a preacher and theologian[16].

We left Edinburgh on the second of June, but before finally taking leave of it, some general observations may be inserted.

The New Town consists of three principal Streets from East to West, said to be a mile in length. Two smaller streets (that is, of smaller houses) run parralel [sic]. The Streets which cross them from N. to S. are strait, wide and regular. The houses are large and good, and tolerably regular, and the streets very spacious. The public buildings are very noble, several with a large Rotunda in the middle. In some of the Streets were high Terraces over the shops. Many of the Shops excel in splendour, particularly Jewellers and Silver smiths. The number of silver urns, and large silver baskets for cakes of all sorts, which are usually brought with the Tea board, is prodigious - besides Castors, Salt cellars and the other articles in plate which are common with us.

Hackney Coaches and Post-chaises are standing in different parts of the Town, and go at reasonable rates. The horses are remarkably good, and when on the Stand are usually covered with a rug. Walking in crowded streets here is particularly unpleasant, from inattention to right and left. Each person goes on his own way, and elbows his neighbour sometimes very uncomfortably.

A 'hackney' was originally a horse for general purposes; not someone's personal steed. In time, a 'hackney' meant a horse available for hire, with or without a 'hackney coach'[17]. Post chaises were carriages hired for a certain distance, from one 'post' to another. A traveller on a long journey - like Mrs Thompson - might hire a series of chaises, each going part of the journey

There is a large proportion of fine, tall, well-shaped and strikingly handsome persons here, especially among the Men. Six foot high is by no means uncommon: and many of the superior females are singularly beautiful. There are at the same time multitudes of short, clumsy and even crippled and deformed people, but fewer of the common middle size than I have observed elsewhere.

We could not reconcile ourselves to the manner of burying the dead, which seems not to be considered as a religious ceremony. We frequently saw a number of well-dressed Men in black, walking together at a brisk pace; and it was some time before we discovered that they were attending a funeral. The coffin is carried by the handles, and is hardly seen when there are about twenty men round it. No woman seems to attend; at least we never saw any. The Grave is prepared, and the Corpse is set down at the side, and is almost immediately lowered by black or black and white cords and Tassels like those of a chamber bell. The earth is then deliberately thrown in, and the attendants draw round the grave, and raising their hats from their heads, bend over the Coffin as tho to take a last farewel [sic], and then turn away, and quietly depart. The whole appeared to us very heathenish, and a blameable neglect of a favourable opportunity of impressing men's minds with the importance of eternal things. I was however informed that it was customary to have some solemn kind of discourse or exhortation before the funeral leaves the house of the deceased; but whether by a minister was not mentioned. It is usual for near relatives to wear muslin cuffs on their coat sleeves, such as fifty years ago were worn in London and known by the name of 'weepers'; but whether at the funeral only, or for some time afterwards, we had no means of judging. Gentlemen in full mourning wear broad crape hatbands tied in large bows, and ends behind.

> *During the 18th century, and probably still in 1807, Scottish funerals were preceded by expensive rituals of watching by the deceased's body, and of eating and drinking before the burial. The minister pronounced a blessing over the feast, but there was no graveside service. Men, but not women, were at the interment[18]. All this confirms what Mrs Thompson saw. She knew London "fifty years ago", having been brought up there.*

Most of the houses we were in were very handsomely furnished, but rather too much crowded; and in many of them the goods seemed to be never rubbed, and seldom dusted. I seldom if ever saw a clean window while I was in Scotland; which neglect the inhabitants excuse on account of the heigth [sic] of many of the windows, and the difficulty of cleaning them with safety. This may have been one cause, but it cannot apply to the ground floors; and it is plain that customary negligence has strengthened into habit.

The beds are covered with white cotton counterpanes, as with us. The Servants take them away at night, and cover the bed with a fine sheet. At the Hotel, our sheets were six yards long; and were first laid down on the bed, and turned back again from the bottom, leaving the feet as in a Pillow cover. The sheet was then turned over the blankets, and spread on the top instead of a Quilt. There were bells to every room in the house, numbered and ticketed according to the number of the room, but this perhaps is customary in large Inns everywhere.

We met with some pleasing instances of interest taken in us as travellers. A principal and very intelligent bookseller, of whom we bought some trifling articles, lent us some volumes of travels thro his country, and drew for us a plan of a fortnight's Tour which he had lately taken on foot, and which we chiefly followed.

> *The bookseller's kindness was one of the things Mrs Thompson recalled in later letters. Writing to her son John, who was back in Edinburgh eighteen months later, she advised him to ask some information from "our good friend the Bookseller, who gave us his pedestrian tour".[19]*

Throughout the whole City of Edinburgh the association of splendour and wretchedness are very striking. The country round is very fine, particularly the south-west quarter where Arthur's Seat, and a beautiful hilly prospect inlivened [sic] with rich groves and pastures, enrich the scene.

I think we were told that there is only one Kirk in Edinburgh which has a ring of bells: St Andrew's in the New Town. Each church in Scotland has one bell to give notice of the time of worship.

There seems to be, in Scotland, a greater dread of appearing to hold particular places or ceremonies sacred, than of falling into carelessness and irreverence. Hats are not taken off on entering the Kirk, and put on at quitting it, with the same decorum as in England. I have observed in some places the men to wear their hats or bonnets till the service begins.

The Version of the Psalms in general use throughout Scotland is an old, un-poetical one that requires great ingenuity in the person who gives out the psalm for singing: and we often admired at the skill with which the Minister modulated those harsh lines in reading so as to drop the superfluous feet, and eke out those which are deficient. The Precentor, as the Clerk is always called, sings the first line alone; and the congregation catch the concluding note and join him in singing the second line; and so to the conclusion.

I forget whether it was in Edinburgh or Glasgow (perhaps in both) that small bunches of coarse grass are kept for sale, about as much as could be clasped in a Man's hand. These seem to be the principal feed of the horses which ply in the streets, or draw the small carts which are so common there. I never saw pattens or any trace of them in Scotland, except in a single mark of a patten ring near the public wash house in Glasgow, where perhaps the women stood to wash in Pattens; but certainly they are very little used.

Many of these heterogeneous kind of remarks may seem but ill-assorted, or scarcely worth mentioning; but as some of the peculiarities of an interesting country they may be curious; and it is not easy to know where to place them better.

Edinburgh from Calton Hill (T. H. Shepherd, 1827)
The view along Princes Street, with the Old Town on the left and the New on the right

"By Lochs and Craggs"
2-9 June

2nd June. We rode thro a pleasant and well cultivated country to Linlithgow, and Falkirk. Proceeding northward, we saw more and more of Highland peculiarities. Plaids began to appear and Tartan dresses, tho not very generally: and sometimes we saw men with a kind of Herding[?] bag thrown over the shoulders in the manner of a Plaid; which is not worn as with us in the form of a Cloak, but twisted round one arm, and thrown over the shoulder, and the opposite end brought under the other arm. Even decent, and sometimes smart women walk on the road with their shoes and stockings in a handkerchief, and their bonnet in their hand; which must be from being accustomed to consider these things as incumbrances, and only to be worn as a kind of dress, for the bonnet at least must be more spoiled in carrying than it would be in wearing.

Leaving Edinburgh, Mrs Thompson is alert for "Highland peculiarities", though Linlithgow and Falkirk are still south of the Forth. The garment "twisted round the arm", however, seems to describe the plaid.

At Linlithgow we went over the old church where James of Scotland saw, as they told us, the spectre who warned him of his defeat at Flodden field, and also the Palace where Mary Stewart was born.

"Tis now the Raven's black abode
Tis now the Apartment of the Toad."

The remains of both those buildings are magnificent.

Warned by a spectre or not, James IV of Scotland was certainly killed at Flodden in 1513 while his wife, sister of Henry VIII of England, waited in Linlithgow Palace. "Mary Stewart" was born there in 1542, becoming Mary Queen of Scots when her father, James V, died one week later.[1]

The town of Falkirk is inhabited principally by Shoemakers, who work in the upper story of their small dwellings; and it was curious to see men working with their heads above the roof, sitting half way out of a small window in it. We lodged here not very comfortably, the Inn being the dirtiest, and with the worst accommodations [sic] we met with in Scotland. No shops were open on the day we left Falkirk, it being a Fast-day preparatory to the Sacrt. [Sacrament] in that place. These solemnities are kept very strictly, about twice in the year, in every part of Scotland; but not on the same day. We soon got beyond the district in which the present Fast was observed; but we met country people coming in their better cloaths for several miles around, who we supposed were going up to the Kirk at Falkirk. The country was flatter than most we have seen lately, but fertile and well-improved.

Shoemaking was a main industry of Falkirk in 1807, though its Library today has no record of workers "with their heads above the roof". Bonnie Prince Charlie, in fact, slept in a bootmaker's shop at Falkirk at the time of his victory there prior to Culloden[2].
A "fast day" was kept at each parish church in Scotland on a weekday prior to the Communion, and was considered to be an important preparation for Communion.[3]

At Stirling we climbed the Castle Hill and saw the old Palace, with some well-carved figures, but more grotesque and uncouth ones. It is now used for Barracks, as is the royal chapel for a store house. The country round was picturesque and fine, and we gained some glimpses of the novelties of Highland scenery. Ben Ledi, and the surrounding mountains, rose in barren Grandeur, and the outline was amazingly diversified. Several beautiful streams, beside the Forth, were in sight. After dinner we proceeded thro a beautiful and romantic country to Callander. The hills, as we approached them, appeared more barren, and less lofty as we became more elevated. The scenery in these parts, I should think, could hardly be exceeded. Plantations, Pastures and Arable land on every side; but scarce any orchards, tho many of the Cottages have neat little gardens, or rather spots cultivated for domestic use. Ornamental gardening seems unthought of. The Corn etc appeared very differently in different places. There was more industry manifested in these parts than in many others we had passed thro. Many women were working in the fields with hoes, and others were sitting sewing in the sun, with their children round them. Many boys were in Tartan bonnets, and some of the smaller ones were in plaid skirts or Fillebegs. Most of the men wore blue bonnets, especially the older ones. The older women throughout Scotland frequently wear large grey cloaks nearly as long as their skirts, and with the Hood up instead of a bonnet. Today some scarlet cloaks appeared. The people in general looked cleaner than nearer Edinburgh. They have Fowls, vegetables etc of their own growth, and the Cottages are often very neat. We saw few tiled houses. The better sort, and even many cottages, were covered with blue slate; and the poorer sort were thatched. There were many neat, and some very superb, mansions in our road.

"Stirling and its castle, in respect of situation, is a miniature of Edinburgh; from the top of the castle is the finest view in Scotland", wrote Pennant in 1769[4]. The view certainly reaches Ben Ledi, beyond Callander, and the road to Callander still passes large houses and estates, which in 1807 would have employed many "cottagers". The small boys' "fillebegs" were what is today the kilt, as compared with the plaid, which wrapped round the whole body.

We arrived at Callander 4 June, a neat pleasant village nearly surrounded by mountains, of which Ben Ledi is the highest. In moist weather it is covered with clouds, and reminded me of the aweful appearance of Mount Sinai at the giving of the Law. Loch Kettarine, about ten miles to the westward, is a fine expanse of water, and is said to be in some parts an hundred fathoms deep, tho in others the Herdsmen drive their cattle thro it. Small Islands covered with Trees are interspersed. The Rocks around the Lake are clothed with Shrubs and small birch Trees, and the whole had a very beautiful appearance. Prodigious masses of Granite were embroidered with grey Lichen; some very curious and uncommon.

Ben Ledi ('hill of God' in Gaelic) reminded Mrs Thompson of Mount Sinai where God gave Moses the Ten Commandments. Loch Katrine was sufficiently well known for her to make a diversion to it in 1807. Scott's 'Lady of the Lake', published in 1810, made many others follow. Dorothy Wordsworth had been there in 1803, approaching it from Loch Lomond, but her description was published much later.[5]

An intelligent Highlander guided us two or three miles round the borders of the Lake, which is of considerable extent. We dined in a little rustic bower, made for the accommodation of Travellers, on such food as we had brought with us. Our path-way was chiefly solid rock, and tho fatigued, we were much gratified with our excursion. We did not sail in the Lake, as they had only one boat, and that was fresh painted.

The cottages in Callander, and Kilmahog the next village, are in general very poor. Making and bleaching cloth are the ordinary occupations. The river Teith runs in a small stream thro Callander, and the water is delightful. The inhabitants appear to retain a good degree of pastoral simplicity. They are very courteous to strangers, and more intelligent than might be expected from their secluded state. I talked with a poor woman who answered all my inquiries with great civility, and then said "Come into my house and drink some milk, an it be your wull". She said her little boy of eight years old was a fine scholar, being in counting [sic], but that learning was very dear: two shillings a quarter. She accepted a shilling without any expression of pleasure, but gave it to her boy and ordered him to thank me. Near her house was a large bell fixed up by the road side in a very high frame, which she said was to give notice when funerals passed by; the only ceremony of the kind I ever observed in Scotland.

Sunday Dress in 1807, from James Hall's 'Travels'
There was no bridge at Kirkmichael near Tomitoul[6]
Churchgoers crossed the river on stilts.

6 June. We went over a mountainous country by Lochs and Craggs to Crieff. In going thro the country in the neighbourhood of Comrie, we went over a wide sort of Common where it is probable there had once been an encampment. Several artificial Hills or Tumuli were in it; and somewhere thereabouts I saw, with great surprize [sic], a small country Church with a Cross near one end. I could not be mistaken - the wonder is that it shd. have survived the fury of Scottish reformation.

The modern traveller still drives from Callander to Crieff "by Lochs and Craggs", passing Loch Lubnaig, Strathyre of Rob Roy fame, and Loch Earn. The church in old "encampment" surroundings was probably the pre-reformation chapel of Dundurn, still existing as a ruin east of St Fillans. It was the burial place of the Stewarts of Ardvorlich, who perhaps erected the unexpected cross.[7]

We drank Tea that afternoon in a very poor Inn at Comrie, and went into the Kirk, which is a large new building, well finished in the Scottish style, of unpainted Fir etc. But it was uncommonly dirty; and on our remarking this to a woman who attended us, she seemed surprised, and said "it was always swept once a month". The solitary bell was on the outside, and distinct from the Church as is frequent in Scotland, and the Boys were amusing themselves with gingling [sic] it.

The writer had recently seen a "bell distinct from the church" at Callander; and 'Annals of the Parish' describes a church whose bell hung from a tree until it blew down, whereupon a steeple was built for the purpose.[8]

The next day, at Crieff, we attended the Kirk - a large unfinished building, without plaster or under-drawing: not from being new, as there appeared no intention to make it better. It was more dirty than many Stables. Service begun at 1/2 past eleven.

This church had been proposed in 1776 to replace an older one; resisted on grounds of cost; debated before judges; and finally begun. But the builder claimed he was losing money, so "it remained unfinished for forty years" - as Mrs Thompson found it in 1807.[9]

The Church was well filled, and an old Minister, of the name of Stirling, preached a preparatory sermon for the Sacrament, which was to be administered three weeks afterwards. He began the service with singing and prayer; and after preaching a considerable time, he sang and prayed anew, then began again from the same text. The whole service lasted about two hours and a half. Before the congregation separated, the minister admonished an Offender; but whether male or female we could not tell. After speaking very forcibly on the heinousness of unchastity, and urging to repentance and reformation, he concluded with our Saviour's words on a similar occasion, 'Go and sin no more, lest a worse thing come upon thee'. Before the Service commenced, or the Minister entered, the Precentor gave notice for the second time of the intended marriage of two persons then named.

> *In the ceremony of admonition the offender, usually sitting on a 'stool of repentance', was publicly rebuked before being restored to church membership; but in this case he or she may not have been present, since Mrs Thompson does not know if it was a man or woman[10]. James Hall, at this time, observed that many ministers were giving up public admonition because fear of it was leading to "child murder" of illegitimately conceived babies[11]; and in Galt's 'Annals of the Parish' the kirk session of 1804 made monetary fines an alternative to "standing in the kirk"[12].*

The Church was full, and a considerable number of the hearers had octavo Bibles, in which they followed the Minster in his proofs. So general it was that the turning over the leaves altogether [ie all together] was distinctly heard. There were many scores of women without bonnets, with tartan plaids wrapped about them in the manner of a long Shawl. They were of different colours and patterns, about a yard in breadth and perhaps two yards or more in length. The appearance of these highland Dames was to me quite singular, but at the same time very respectable. The rest of their dress was generally a printed calico Gown, and a checked apron. The men had no distinction, except that many had bonnets, but no Plaids. They kept their heads covered till service began, which is frequently seen in Scotland. In the afternoon, the son of the old Minister preached.

> *The older Mr Stirling, sixty seven years old at this time, had been minister at Crieff since 1770. His son Michael, aged twenty seven, had the parish of Cargill.[13]*

Both Father and Son prayed evangelically and preached the leading truths of the Gospel with some clearness; yet something seemed wanting both in preacher and people. There was a strange mixture - a degree of attention which seemed to bespeak some spiritual understanding; and yet a striking want of solemnity. The most flagrant indecorum is the handing snuff-boxes about, which we first observed here, though we afterwards saw it in other parts of Scotland. Perhaps much of what appears to us to be irreverence may proceed from reluctance to attribute sacredness to a Place. No act of devotion is used on entrance: and the general custom which I believe I noticed before, of the whole congregation sitting down when they judge from the Minister's voice or expression that his prayer is drawing to a close, appears to a stranger totally inconsistent with the spirit of worship, because not only the practice is indecent, but it creates a bustle that must necessarily disturb the attention of all around.

In the afternoon we had only one sermon, and when that and the prayer and psalm were concluded by the younger Mr Stirling, the Father came into the pulpit and sat by his son. A pewter bason was fixed on the outside of the pulpit, and we learned that a child was to be baptised. The old Minister gave some very solemn and important advice to the parents of the child, which was then taken up to the pulpit door by by the father, and was sprinkled with water in the name of the Trinity. The younger Mr S than gave the benediction with uplifted hands and great solemnity; and it was peculiarly pleasing to see two ministers, thus nearly related, acting thus in concert.

Crieff baptism records for that day show that the child was "Kath." (probably Katherine), daughter of Donald McNaughton & Charlotte Law[14].
A modern guidebook to Canongate Kirk, Edinburgh, describes, almost in Mrs Thompson's own words, this "old reformed Scottish custom": "The Minister would remain in the pulpit, to which was attached an iron bracket holding a basin, usually pewter but sometimes silver, and he would lean over at the appropriate time to baptise the child, which was held up by the father"[15]. Canongate Kirk retains and uses its iron bracket. The illustration shows a pewter basin, dated 1814, in the Borders.

Pewter baptismal basin, dated 1814, at Ettrick Kirk.

In the evening I found out a pious Missionary, who usually speaks to the people in Gaelic, which many of them understand better than english. At this time however he spoke in english; and much that he gave was the sincere milk of the Word; tho dashed with the most violent and injudicious sentiments of final perseverance that I ever heard. His audience was small, and appeared to want rousing rather than this kind of lulling doctrine. The preacher kept a small stationer's shop and appeared to be very low in the World, and glad to meet with a little countenance and encouragement.

It seems illogical that "violent sentiments" should "lull" audience; but final perseverance had a particular meaning. The majority of Christians believe they should combine faith in God with Christian actions. Some Calvinists, including the Missionary, believed that those chosen by God for salvation had nothing further to do.[16] That was the view which Burns satirised in 'Holy Willie's Prayer'.[17] That was what Mrs Thompson, far more traditional than Burns, attacked as a "lulling doctrine".

From Crieff we travelled to Perth on the 8th of June, thro an open, cultivated country with mountains in sight, tho none near. Many of the habitations appeared extremely wretched, and no very good ones came in our view, tho some of the Farms seemed to be considerable. We had the usual sight of indolence and scanty clothing; great boys lounging about, sometimes attending a solitary cow. We saw no Highland dresses here.

The writer seems tired in this section of the journey, commenting on the "usual" indolence in this paragraph and the "usual" shallow rivers in the next, when she does not mention them elsewhere.

Perth is a handsome Town, in a fine open country, and the general appearance was reviving after passing thro so much rocky country. A bridge of ten arches crossed a stream of the usual shallowness. We saw some tiers of Bricks, and a few brick houses which looked lively after the succession of dirty grey buildings. Our Inn was dull and incommodious, and the weather unfavourable for walking about. We therefore proceeded to Dunkeld, thro as barren a country as most we have met with in Scotland. Most of the lands were either quite bare - a coarse clay, or strong soil - or else grown over with broom. In the neighbourhood of Birnham-wood the prospect improved, and we had many trees arround [sic] us, tho of small growth. A good deal of Industry was displayed in some parts; particularly in one little district where a few houses of the lowest description were placed in the midst of a mile or two of well cultivated plain, extending in a slip of perhaps half a mile broad, with pretty high rocks behind and before.

Perth, so briefly described here as a "handsome town", had a thriving history, academic institutions and manufactures, as described in James Hall's 'Travels'[18]. It did not detain Mrs Thompson, however, and nor did Birnam Wood, so significant in Shakespeare's 'Macbeth'. Birnam Wood is close to Inver Inn and Dunkeld.

We reached Inver Inn to Tea; and the next morning walked over part of the Duke of Athol's grounds, said to be 6000 acres in extent. A thin soil covered the solid rock, and a winding path is cut thro it in different directions. A great variety of fine trees, and some rare ones, are exhibited. The Mansion was not noble, nor did we see the inside. A new one in very superior style is preparing. We saw in the grounds some Roebuck fawns, which were not so shy as might have been expected, or as they probably will be when they are older.

These grounds are at Dunkeld House, which was a winter house of the Duke in 1807 (his main residence being Blair Atholl Castle, fifteen miles away). The House was pulled down in 1828 without being rebuilt. Its woodland had been planted in the late 18th century with trees from Britain, Europe and America.[19]

Many convenient shelters of the rustic kind are placed in different parts of the walk. but the greatest curiosity is Ossian's Cave, which appears to be modern: a kind of Temple, rather large, and handsome, into which strangers enter without any particular expectation except of a commodious resting place. We were shewn into a room adorned with Shells and Mirrors; and a large painting of Ossian and his Dogs, and three female figures who seem to be listening to the old Bard's strains. While we were surveying it our guide, unperceived by us, drew a string, and the whole door, or perhaps the side of the room on which the picture was placed, drew inwards, and introduced us to a much larger room, covered with mirrors on every side, and a large window opening onto a tremendous cataract whose waters rushed down in three large streams, over points and crags that sent it in every direction, rushing dashing and foaming with a noise that was almost deafening. The astonishing effect cannot easily be described; and our old man shut us in to enjoy the scene as long as we pleased. What added to the singularity was that the mirrors were so disposed as to reflect the cascade to the greatest advantage: and those on the ceiling reflected the stream as inverted, so that the water appeared ascending - gushing, bubbling and boiling like a mighty cauldron.

The writer's long, descriptive sentences reflect her excitement at the scene. The building, usually called 'Ossian's Hall', was a summerhouse built by Lord John Murray in 1757, before he became Duke of Atholl. It had an outer and an inner room.[20] In 1769 Pennant described window panes painted red, "which makes the water resemble a fiery cataract".[21] In 1783 the intervening door was painted with a picture of Ossian, and mirrors were fitted which made the water seem to pour in all directions. Wordsworth disapproved when he saw it, but others were delighted. 'Ossian's Hall' was blown up, in 1869, by protestors against tolls payable to the Duke for use of the bridge in Dunkeld. It was rebuilt in its present simplified state by the architect Basil Spence in 1951[22].

Ossian's Hall, Dunkeld, as seen today

Ossian was a legendary hero of the third century court of Tara. Writings attributed to him had been 'translated' and published by James Macpherson (died 1796), but Gaelic experts had discredited Macpherson's work in 1797.[23]

Scotland justly ranks amongst the countries of superior beauty; and it has many peculiarities; but if I was to denominate it from any single circumstance, I should call it the land of Lichens. Never did I see an approach towards the quantity of that vegetable, which appears to thrive so much more in this country. I shall learn to give more credit in future to those who enlarge on a given subject. I had

53

supposed that the writers on Botany multiplied this species, from its accidental varieties; but really the kinds here are so numerous, and so strongly marked, that I no longer hesitate to believe there may be as great a variety as is represented. Every rock and Tree is embroidered with one sort or another, and sometimes with two or three sorts together, and the Lichens are often to be distinguished to a considerable distance. Some adhere so closely that no art can separate them. Of others, the fronds spread loosely over a large surface, and only the stems or roots adhere. But the most amazing circumstance is in the case of many of the Trees in the Duke of Athol's pleasure grounds. The bark of many of the trees, particularly Firs and Larches, whose branches rise from the bottom, were so covered with Lichens as to appear as tho covered with Snow. This parasitical vegetation seems to destroy the branches it covers, tho the top of the Tree frequently appears in full vigour. There were I suppose many hundreds of Trees loaded thus with Lichens; and in the state of partial death which I have described.

> *Scotland seems less a "land of lichens" today. Atmospheric pollution reduced them in the Forth-Clyde belt; but they flourish as in 1807 at Blair Atholl.[24]*

On the 9th of June we returned to Dunkeld thro Perth [probably "from Dunkeld, through Perth"], and in the evening we reached Kinross. We walked to the side of Loch Leven, but too late to see it to advantage; and the boats which are daily employed in fishing were put up for the Night. We saw at a distance the ruins of the Castle in which poor Queen Mary was confined for some months. The little Island on which it stands appears but of few acres extent, and the Castle could not have been large. The Island was covered with high Trees, and the whole had a very picturesque appearance; but unless the distance was much greater than it appeared, the situation must have been a confined one for a Palace.

> *Antonia Fraser comments that Castle Island, now barely 300 yards long, was still smaller in Mary Queen of Scots' day (and presumably in 1807), because the water of Loch Leven was higher.[25] "Poor Queen Mary" was there for nearly a year in 1567-8. There she miscarried twins fathered by Bothwell, and there she was forced to abdicate the Scottish throne in favour of her thirteen month old son, James VI. She escaped the island, and an army rallied to her help, but was defeated near Glasgow. Mary fled to England, where she was beheaded nineteen years later.*

We lodged at an excellent Inn at Kinross Green, and proceeded the next day by Alloa to Cumbernauld old(?) House, and the following [day] we arrived in Glasgow.

> *Perhaps there was no time to visit Alloa. It was a populous town in 1807, with a deep water harbour on the River Forth. It produced quantities of serge, linen and muslin, and it shipped its coal, and glass bottles, as far as Denmark, Germany and Portugal.[26]*

"Greatly delighted with Glasgow"
10-21 June

At Glasgow, we were greatly delighted with the display of comfort and industry. The houses and public buildings were extremely good, and the streets spacious, strait and regular. We staid about a fortnight here, and found everything as desirable as so large and populous a place could furnish. The views round the City were delightfully interesting, from their fruitfulness and high cultivation, as well as from their natural situation.

Pennant, in 1769, had called Glasgow "the best of any modern second rate city I ever saw"[1]. But a map in Denholm's 'History of Glasgow' (1804)[2], and another by Fleming (1808), show the expansion, in those four years alone, into new areas of "spacious, strait and regular streets", surrounded by new farms to supply the growing city, and by the country residences of city men.

The Canals are well worthy of observation; and the Aqueduct Bridge is reckoned a stupendous work, the Canal crossing the river at a great heigth [sic]. But as the Canal cannot be seen at the same time with the river below, it is not easy to enter into the whole of the curiosity at once, which therefore appears less wonderful than it really is.

The Forth and Clyde Canal, linking the North Sea with the Atlantic, was already considered a wonder; and now its Aqueduct Bridge carried the Canal high over the river Kelvin, north west of Glasgow.[3] Mrs Thompson was disappointed with the Bridge; but its foundation stone (1787) says it was "supposed the largest fabric of its kind in the World"[4].

The Aqueduct Bridge, Glasgow
(Early 19th century print)

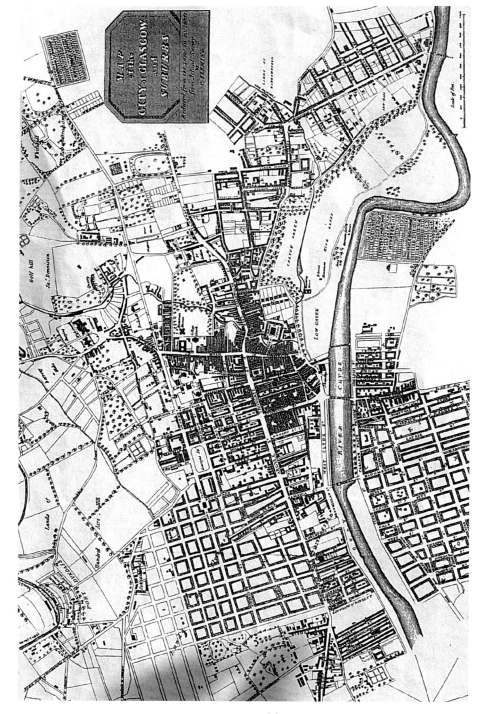

Fleming's map of Glasgow (1808)

The Wash house is shown near Low Green. The canal is at the top of the map

It is a pleasant walk to the Quarry Town; and indeed the whole surrounding countryside is so beautifully diversified with pleasant houses, from the rich Manufacturer's Villa to the humblest Cottage that can be commodious, and the grounds are so well improved either in Bleach-yards, or Print-fields, or pasture grounds etc, that the eye cannot soon be weary of surveying.

The "Quarry Town" may be just one of several quarries then supplying the expanding city. Bleachyards and printfields were the province of numerous workers, many of them women and children, who worked on the cotton cloth woven in the city.[5]

In a large open Space about a Mile out of the City is a Building fitted up as a common Wash house, where the Inhabitants send their servants to wash the family linnen. The heigth [sic] of the houses, and not being accommodated with yards at home, may in part account for this odd custom. But nothing of the kind is practised in Edinburgh, where the houses are still higher, and in general more crowded. It is said to be very injurious to the Servants who mix there with all sorts of Gossips, and many worthless people; but we were told by a respectable house keeper that she should not be able to get a Servant to live with her if she did not allow of washing in the public Washouse [sic] a few times in the year. We looked in with some apprehension, and saw a strange assemblage of Tubs, Coppers, wet and dirty linnen, and washers of all ages. Of course the clamour was great; but we met with no incivility. On this Grass in different patches of the large Close in which this Institution is held, the clothes are dried; and a great number of Women and children are employed in the washhouse, and in watching [sic] the Linnen.

The Wash house gave the city £300-£400 per annum from the small amounts paid by citizens for the use of its facilities.[6]

We were aware that it was not necessary to travel into Scotland to see manufactories [sic]; but when we were amongst them, we were not likely to see them to so much advantage elsewhere. We saw several in Glasgow; tho but little of the Cotton manufactories, which the proprietors are either not fond of shewing, or some accidental reasons prevented us. One curious part of the process in making Muslin we were shewn by a friend. After the Muslin is wove [sic], it is drawn with great rapidity over a large iron cylinder, glowing like a hot heater, to singe off the loose down and hairs. It might be expected that the whole should be in a blaze; and the hissing is very loud, I think attended with sparks; and it is much discoloured, but not otherwise injured.

The word "manufactory" was more used in the early 19th century than "factory". It is possible that the shyness of cotton manufacturers to show their places of work resulted from criticism, which was now growing, of their use of child labour.

We saw the whole process of making and colouring earthen ware, which, as it was new to us, was curious and interesting. A little boy was painting a small Plate in a pattern and colour that I thought by no means improved its appearance, but he both held it and worked on it with an air and dexterity that diverted us greatly. One, a few years older, shewed us the process of making the better sort of Tea-pots in form of a boat, which I think he made on a mould, slicing the Clay and joining the seams much as we close a pie. In another room men, women and children were employed in finishing large Beer Jugs. One or two children were cutting the patterns, which were printed on a very thin kind of transparent paper. The women fixed them on with a kind of size, and then men, I believe, set them to harden in a kind of oven; but I have forgotten all further particulars.

Mrs Thompson's husband, as a merchant, would have been interested in Hall's comment of 1807: "The prosperity of Glasgow is truly astonishing. It was thought that it would decline when we lost America, but when the merchants and manufacturers found themselves shut out of the American market, they studiously looked for another. When prevented from importing tobacco to gratify the propensities of the gentlemen, they imported cottons &c. from the West Indies; and, working these up into elegant fabrics, gratified the taste of the ladies. Thus they did good to their country, and put the money into the Scotch, that used to go into the Gentoo [Indian] weavers pockets."[7] In other words, Glasgow in 1807 was importing raw cotton from the West Indies - and by now from the newly independent United States - and was spinning and weaving it, in Glasgow mills, into the sort of cloth which had once come ready-made from India.)[8]

"An excursion into the Highlands"
From 22 June

On the 22 June we made an excursion for a few days into the Highlands.

The "excursion", from Glasgow back to Glasgow, seems to have taken about a week. It was possibly the one suggested to Mrs Thompson by the Edinburgh bookseller, who took a fortnight, but did it on foot. In the diary she moves straight from Glasgow to Loch Lomond, but clearly went to Dumbarton on the way, so here is her description of the latter.

We dined at Dumbarton on the 22, and climbed two hundred steps to the Castle to "see" the surrounding prospect in a thick haze, thro which we could hardly discern objects at a hundred yards distance. We had afterwards the most extraordinary sight of a Glass-house. There were three in Dumbarton. The workmen had gone home to dine, but after waiting [for them] with some impatience, we were well repaid. The heat indeed of six furnaces was almost in supportable [sic], and I feared we should have been lastingly the worse for it, especially as we were frequently exposed to a strong current of air; but the process was on the whole truely [sic] interesting. We watched it, from the glass being put into the first furnace till it was finally put up in the annealing Fire. First a Man took a lump of the glass in a semi liquid state out of the glowing Cauldron, on the end of a long iron tube, and turned it round in the furnace (the Cauldron more probably) till it had collected a sufficient quantity. This he turned and rubbed on every side upon a large stone till it had obtained something of a cylindrical form, when he held it for some time in a second furnace and blew strongly thro the tube till it swelled gradually to a considerable size. It was passed thro a succession of Fires, and inflated with air till it became like a very large glass water bottle. In the course of the process it expanded amazingly, and became flat; and a small part which projected where the tube had at first been fixed was struck off by means of water, and a smart stroke of an iron instrument. We saw this glass carried from fire to fire, glowing like hot iron; but when viewed near the Furnace it was going into it appeared perfectly transparent, and no longer red, in comparison of the superior heat. At last it was carried in its extended state, like a small Coach wheel into the annealing Furnace, where it was to remain about fifty hours, when it would be completed.

This is probably a description of the making of sheets of 'crown' or 'bull's eye' glass (so called from the lump left in the glass where the blow pipe had attached) which was used for window panes until the early nineteenth century.[1]

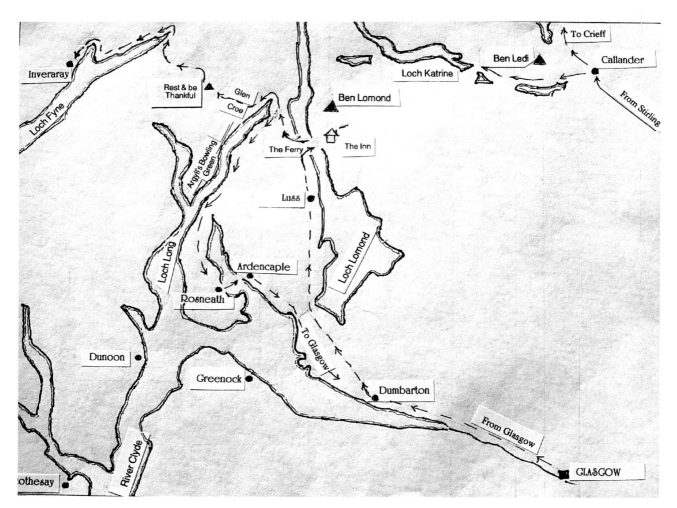

The 'excursion into the Highlands' Glasgow - Inveraray - Glasgow
showing, top right, part of the earlier route north

Dumbarton Castle (right) and glassworks (left)
by I Clark (1824)

The workmen appeared not unhealthy or uncomfortable. They work twelve hours and rest twelve hours at one time, and have thirty six hours work and thirty six hours rest at another. So say my memorandums, which I believe are accurate; tho I confess the inequality of the intervals strikes me at this time as improbable. We were struck with the appearance of the work-men, who were fine, tall, well-proportioned people, and in general remarkably intelligent and obliging; particularly the Foreman, whose manners and conversation were singularly courteous, manly and interesting. He gave us a correct and philosophical explanation of the whole process, and seemed pleased to be listened to with interest. His province seemed to be that of placing the Glass in the annealing furnace, which is probably the hottest - tho one of the others blazed more furiously, reminding of the account given of Nebuchadnezzar's furnace, the flames of which slew all within their reach. This Man, who appeared to give the finish to the work, armed himself with a large double covering over the shoulders, and a sort of cushion or hood on the side of his head to guard against the intense heat. He said they perspired profusely, but seldom got any cold but what sweating would carry off. There were many boys between eight and twelve employed in different ways; and they sung and ran about merrily, as tho they had been playing in the open air.

Nebuchadnezzar's furnace blazed in the Old Testament book of Daniel, chapter 3.

After sleeping at the ill-conducted Inn at Luss, we set out for Ben-Lomond. We rode two or three miles to the Loch; and were ferried over by a fine young highland woman with her hair flowing about her face like a mermaid, and without shoe or stocking. Her brother rented a Farm of £200 pr. annm. [sic], and she, with her Mother and Sisters, conducts family affairs and accommodates strangers who visit the Loch, and it is only occasionally that she plied the oar; which, she said, was not fit for "any (for every) woman". She was very intelligent; said that the Gaelic was little in use among them now, especially amongst young people; but her Mother "had good Gaelic".

Luss, of the "ill-conducted inn", is nowadays a very picturesque village on the west shore of Loch Lomond. Two or three miles northwards, a ferry from Inverbeg still crosses to the Rowardennan Hotel, the 17th century inn which the writer is almost certainly describing, from which one can climb Ben Lomond.

Ben Lomond is very high and rugged, but as I did not attempt to climb it I can give no account from my own observation. I waited in a kind of inn at the bottom while our Party ascended; and as I had the supper [?] room to myself during the absence of a Sportsman, I might have made many remarks [?] on Scottish scenery, manners etc etc if I had been within reach of writing implements, but now they have escaped me.

The mistress of the house appeared unequal to her station, tho I believe she imagined herself above it, and there was an air of dissatisfaction and discomfort about everything around her that would not have been the case with a true highlander. This woman was a foreigner, that is a Borderer, or native of the Lowlands. She was young, and I gathered from her that she had wed her Laddie with high expectations of felicity, but, finding much labour and scanty means, she had grown careless and dejected. I asked after books; but they seemed a commodity little in request; at least, she said she had one or two godly books, but seemed shy of producing what was so obsolete.

Mrs Thompson had high expectations of Highlanders and was glad that this landlady was not one of them!

I got a scanty dinner, and was glad, after a few hours separation, to rejoin my companions in the former *[i.e. probably "the forementioned"]* Inn, where we found our young Pilot exerting herself more suitably than before. Our travellers were glad to regale on her eggs and Mutton ham, to which we added the refreshment of Tea. She and her brother acquitted themselves with an address that would not have disgraced a superior station; and we shall long remember the name of <u>Margaret Walker</u> with complacency. A poor family dined in this house while we were there, who were emigrating to America. In our return over Loch Lomond we were accompanied by a highland Girl about fifteen, who joined in rowing for the pleasure of it; and she and the Lad who was our proper Rower amused themselves with singing Erse [Gaelic] songs and chattering in the same language. She had <u>run over from about seven miles distant</u> to get a Man to assist in taking a shoal of Herrings which had appeared in her Neighbourhood, and had to return the same distance. She walked our pace a little way after we had quitted the boat, and when asked why she had not shoes or stockings on, she said it was too hot, and that she could make more haste without them. She was well-dressed in her fashion - a new green stuff skirt, and tidy bed-gown and shawl, and her locks flowing without hat or confinement. Her companion had seemed very sullen and unsociable while in the Boat, refusing either to join in the amusements of rowing, singing or discussing, tho he was said to understand Erse the best of the crew. I suppose he was tired of her lingering with us on the road, and gave a shrill whistle when a quarter of a mile before us; which she understood, and flew after him like an arrow from a bow.

In William Combe's 'Dr Prosody', an imaginary English clergyman harangues Scotsmen, who wear the blue bonnet, plaid and fillebeg, by Loch Lomond

The usual route to Inveraray left Loch Lomond at Tarbet, going west, past Arrochar, into Glen Croe.[2] The present A83 rises steadily up to the high point at the "Rest and be Thankful" summit, but the road in 1807 followed the valley floor and then zig-zagged to the summit ("One of the most formidable passes in the Highlands, amongst such mountains as must shake the nerves of every timorous person", wrote an English traveller, Sarah Murray, in 1799.[3]) West of the "Rest and be Thankful" the road descends more easily towards Inveraray, which Mrs Thompson here calls "the Highlands".

"Rest and be Thankful"
The old road and (above) today's A83

The greater part of our road to the Highlands was sufficiently dreary and rough. We reached Inveraray to Tea on the 24 [June]; and afterwards went over the Duke of Argyle's Castle, which was at that time in great disorder, being [about] to undergo a thorough repair. Some fine statues - as we judged from their figure - on the staircase were covered over compleatly [sic] with Sheets. The main body of the house is lighted by Sky-lights, and it is surrounded at bottom by the different apartments; and a circular staircase introduces to a Gallery which the Chambers surround in like manner.

We saw a few interesting Portraits, and a great deal of beautiful Tapestry. The furniture, hangings etc were very noble. There are twenty two lodging rooms, beside state apartments, on the ground floor. The Castle is square, with four circular Towers at the corners. The Vestibule goes thro the middle of the building, and forms the Sky lights at top [sic]. The Grounds were extensive and pleasant, and some of the outbuildings were of a singular construction; but it was too late in the evening for us to survey them.

Inveraray Castle is a late 18th century building replacing an older one. "Thorough repair" was therefore not necessary, but both castle and town were constructed between 1770 and 1839 (the period of the 5th and 6th Dukes), so development would have been in progress. Mrs Thompson seems not to have known that four charming portraits of 1784 - the children of the 5th Duke - were by John Opie RA, her cousin's husband. At a later date her nephew, Henry Perronet Briggs RA, would paint the 7th Duke.[4]

Inveraray is a place of uncommon appearance, and has been designed and ornamented so as to make a good object for the Duke's Domain. Built on the side of Loch Fine, it gave me the idea of a Venetian hamlet. The huge hill of Duniquaish [sic] is improved, and attached to the Duke's pleasure grounds, and a small observatory on the Top looks quaintly diminutive on such a mountain. It is opposite to the Inn where we lodged, tho at a great distance. We saw, in an inclosure near the Inn, a monument in memory of Cambels [sic] who were slain there in some popular tumult, now nearly forgotten. It was some centuries ago and we heard the story very obscurely.

The Thompsons' inn, facing the hill of Duniquoich, was probably the present Argyll Hotel. Then called the Great Inn, it had been built at the same time as the 18th century Castle to accommodate guests to the Castle as well as other travellers. The monument, now in the Castle grounds, commemorates seventeen Campbells (the family name of the Dukes of Argyll) killed by the Marquis of Atholl in 1685.

Inveraray town and castle from Duniquoich Hill, by J Clark

Loch Fine is an arm or inlet of the Sea, which it joins thirty miles off. Great quantities of the largest Herrings are caught in the Loch, and the borderers *[presumably, people living on the border of the Loch]* are chiefly fishermen. Most of the hills arround [sic] are barren; but the low grounds are industriously cultivated where capable.

We returned by Roseneath and Ardencaple to Glasgow, along the Military road on Glen Crose which was cut through a great extent of rock by the English soldiers after the last Rebellion, to facilitate an intercourse with the Highlands. A large range of Mountains near Inveraray is called 'Argyle's Bowling Green', in reference to the uncommon ruggedness of their summits. They appear only fit for the residence of ... rns [?]; and I should suppose the most desperate circumstances that had ever occurred in the Highlands had never induced human creatures to take up their abode there.

> *This is certainly a brief description of the return to Glasgow, but it indicates the route taken. From Inveraray they returned to the Rest and be Thankful summit. (The poet Keats, seeing 'Rest and be Thankful' on his map in 1818, thought it must be an inn where he could have breakfast. Sadly, it was only the top of a hill).[5] After following the Glen Croe road - built after the 1745 Jacobite "Rebellion" - almost back to Loch Lomond, they turned south west at Arrochar on today's A814. After seeing the crags of "Argyle's Bowling Green" on the other side of Loch Long, they continued southwards on the west shore of Gare Loch. At Rosneath they took the ferry to Ardencaple, near Rhu, and drove on to Glasgow.*

Former road bridge on the Thompsons' route to Inveraray
with Loch Fyne in the background

New industries and an old Saint
29 June - 9 July

After this steep and rugged Journey we had delight in again returning to the comforts of Glasgow, where we staid a few days, and then bent our course southward. But before I take leave intirely [sic] of this much-admired place I will add two or three things which were omitted in their proper situation. The first two days we passed at Glasgow we lodged at a Hotel; and being anxious to get private lodgings before the Sunday, I prowled about the City with weary feet, and found my fatigue greatly increased by the odd circumstances I am going to relate. It is customary for those who let lodgings in Glasgow - I never saw it any where else - to hang out a square board, on which is painted in distinct characters "THIS FLAT (or so many rooms in it) TO LET". These are called Tokens, and are to be seen, at one storey or another, perhaps almost every tenth house, at least in the trading part of the Town. The inhabitants of the different <u>Flats</u>, both here and in Edinburgh, are as little acquainted with their Neighbours above or below them as persons living in London are with their next door Neighbours; and when I inquired, at the shop on the ground floor, about apartments on the second or third story, they knew no more of the inhabitants, or whether the apartments were at liberty, than tho they had lived in another Street: so that I was obliged to climb upstairs, and frequently had the mortification to find that the Lodgings were full - tho the Notice was not removed. Another peculiarity is in the construction of the houses in Glasgow, which usually have (at least in the middling kind of houses) a circular apendage [sic] fixed at one corner, rising from the bottom to the top, and called a Turnpike: in the interior of which is the staircase, so that you ascend from one story to another without necessarily entering the house at all.

During our stay in Glasgow, we one day took one of the long coaches for Paisley, where we saw more of the Muslin manufacture than we had met with before. They were chiefly employed in the fancy way at Paisley; at least what we saw was principally Leno's [?] and flowered and spotted articles, part of which was done with the needle. We saw two decent women working at a window and stopped on the outside to look at them. They opened the window (which certainly did not seem much accustomed to the operation), and with the greatest courtesy described the process to us. Indeed I must do the Caledonians the justice to say I never saw anything of the surliness, or sneering disposition amongst them, to which the lower class of John Bull's children are so subject. In a very few instances that we met with churlishness in Scotland, I verily believe the offenders were not Scots.

We saw the old Gothic Chapel at Paisley, which contains some remains of royalty: one stone in particular on a Queen who, from the circumstances of her son being born with a blind eye, has always been distinguished by the name of Blear-eye. This Chapel is celebrated for its remarkable echo; but of this we were too modest to avail ourselves by singing as we were desired. We heard, however, the echo from shutting the large door, which was loud and formidable, and I think reverberated.

Much of Paisley Abbey was in ruins from the early 16th to the late 19th century, when restoration began. The "old Gothic Chapel" of St Mirin was intact when Mrs Thompson was there. Separated by a wall from the main building, its echo was well known. Today the wall has gone, and the echo has gone with it.

The "Queen" was a princess. Marjorie, daughter of King Robert the Bruce, married Walter Stewart. Their son Robert II, the first Stewart king of Scotland, had discoloured eyes and was nicknamed "Blear-eye": but Marjorie's own grave in St Mirin's chapel was sometimes called "Queen Bleary's tomb".[1]

We proceeded Southward by the Falls of the Clyde, but found them inferior to our expectation, owing principally perhaps to the dryness of the Season. The rocky bed of one of them was sufficient to make a most stupendous display when there was plenty of water. Even as it was, the appearance was beyond most that we have seen, having a resemblance to the Stridd at Bolton in Craven, but on a ten-fold larger scale. Scotland abounds in Cataracts; and almost every hill side sends forth a rill or two, which even in this general scantiness of water formed little cascades which greatly embellished the prospect.

At the Strid, near Bolton Abbey in Yorkshire, the river Wharfe rushes through a narrow channel in which many have drowned; but the Falls of Clyde are far bigger. "About three miles above Lanark", wrote James Hall, also in 1807, "the Clyde, the greatest river in Scotland next to the Tay, tumbles, in one cataract, from rock to rock, for about the space of a mile. I am really at a loss how to describe the effect produced by those tremendous cascades".[2]

At Lanark we viewed the Cotton Mills, which are built like a little Town, and have a striking tho irregular appearance. Strangers are not admitted: the reason given is the great waste of time to the people employed.

The "little Town" is now the New Lanark World Heritage Village. The cotton mill there, powered by the river Clyde, was the largest in Scotland when Robert Owen became its manager in 1800. In the next few years, which included the time of Mrs Thompson's visit, the business was building up to high profitability. From about 1813 Owen embarked on radical schemes for fair wages, good housing for his workers, and enlightened children's education, which included singing and dancing. Inevitably, Owen was criticised by reactionary people. In 1816 Mrs Thompson's husband described Owen as "a wild theorist" after hearing scandalous reports of him in Parliament. Today, most people would say he was far in advance of his time.[3]

It seems likely that "strangers were not admitted" in 1807 because that was when the mill was being developed to full capacity.[4]

Progressive education at New Lanark
Print by by G Hunt (1825)

We passed thro Hamilton and went over the palace of the Duke of that Title. It was an old building, but without anything of the venerable. The rooms were very low, and nothing in them rests in my memory except the very fine picture of Daniel in the Lions' Den, by Reubens.

Hamilton Palace - now demolished because of coal-mining subsidence - reached its full magnificence in the 1820s, but it should have been impressive in 1807. Dorothy Wordsworth called it "without grandeur, a heavy, lumpish mass"[5] - after she had been refused admittance! At least Mrs Thompson saw the famous Rubens, now in Washington D.C. It is famous for the realism of its menacing lions.[6]

We went some miles out of our road to visit Wilson Town, where there are large Iron works. The place had a most dreary appearance. Scarce a Tree or vegetable of any kind was to be seen, and except the residence of one of the Proprietors, the houses were very poor, and occupied by the Miners and Smiths. The Manager told us it was the best Ore in Britain; and that 60 Ton pr. Week could be wrought at one Furnace. They have five Furnaces, but little was doing at that time, I think for want of Water. They have only Land Carriage to Edinburgh or Glasgow, and pay 15/- [15 shillings] pr. Ton. It is 28 Miles to Leith, where Water Carriage begins. They pay £600 pr. week in Wages and the Iron is worth £9 pr. Ton.

Wilsontown, a small place today, is on the A706, north of Forth. It developed from 1779, when three brothers Wilson joined together to develop coal and ironstone resources in the area. By 1804 blast furnaces and a rolling mill, water and steam power, gave employment to nearly 500 men: but financial disagreements and heavy debt led to the liquidation of the Company in 1813.[7]

Former engine house at Wilsontown, photographed in 1960

26 June, we left Douglas Mill and travelled thro a most dreary road to Moffatt, which we reached in the Eveng. The Town is neat and lively, situated in a Bottom surrounded by moderately high hills, most of which in that Neighbourhood are cultivated and woody.

The inn at Douglas Mill, at the junction of roads from Edinburgh, Ayr, Glasgow and Carlisle, was known then as "a very comfortable halt where horses could be changed, and repairs receive attention, while travellers refreshed themselves before proceeding farther on their journey".[8] Mrs Thompson may have stayed overnight. The 25 miles on to Moffat looks fascinating on Forrest's 1816 survey map of Lanark, going through towns and villages both on and off today's roads, passing the estates of this and that landowner, with views of hills where lead was mined and "gold formerly wrought".[9] But perhaps it seemed "most dreary" because

70

it twisted and turned, climbing close to today's Beattock Summit, and crossing another watershed before it dropped into the "Bottom" where Moffat lies.

The Kirk and many of the houses were built of a greyish stone and ornamented with red brick. Every door and window had a bordering of different colour from the houses, which gave the Town a pretty and uncommon appearance. The mineral spring for which Moffatt is famed is of the nature of Harrogate Water; but so much weaker in quality that it is said to require two scotch pints, which is two english quarts, to produce the proper effect. Besides, the Well is rather too far off for a Walk, and there is no accommodation or Shelter when there.

The Kirk of that day has gone, but many houses survive in grey stone with red sandstone decoration. The mineral spring shown in these illustrations is a good uphill walk from the town. It, and another in the hills some miles away, were famous for their chalybeate (iron-bearing) water, which doctors later in the century said could be exported to British India without deterioration.[10]

On Sunday we attended twice at the [Moffat] Kirk, where a plain faithful Preacher delivered the truths of the Gospel with loving earnestness. Being in want of something to read I called one day on this Minister, Revd Mr Johnstone, and found him pious and friendly, with the success of the gospel much at heart. He lamented the degree of formality that was amongst his people: a few of them, however, give him comfort. He had once been in England, and was astonished to find religious people there - Ministers and others - talking about Christian experience, and conversing on religious subjects, as customary matters. All which freedom seems banished from the cautious discourse of these wary Scotts [sic].

I visited afterwards an old Saint who appeared just on the wing for Heaven. She was known by the name of old Grizzel, and belonged to a congregation of Cameronians, none of whom, excepting her own family, lived within thirty miles of her. I could hardly understand her dying accents and broad scotch dialect; yet we seemed mutually comforted together in the injoyment [sic] of the same faith, and the hope of reaching the same glorious Kingdom.

The Cameronians, followers of Richard Cameron (died 1680) were extreme Covenanters who refused to be included in any Kirk established by law. From 1743 they became the Reformed Presbyterian Church: some congregations still remain.[11] The Cameronian Regiment (founded 1689, disbanded 1968) was first recruited from followers of Cameron.

The Manse is a very neat and comfortable building, tho rather small for a family with six children. The Kirk sends up its tall red steeple, and radiant spire, in the midst of some tall fine Trees which embower it. The burying Ground is at some distance, and, like most of the scotch Church-Yards, shut up from common observation.

We found throughout Scotland excellent Bread and excellent Water. We did not meet with any household bread: nothing seemed in use but the best wheaten bread, except in the Highlands where Oat Bread is eaten by the Poor, and lower classes.

We were not conscious of any difference of Climate. The weather was often very hot, and much as it might be expected to be further South. One remarkable circumstance occurred while we were in Edinburgh which was quite new to us, and we were told it foreboded great heat. About six o'clock in the evening on the 21st May, after a clear Day with cold easterly wind, a mist descended which intirely [sic] obscured the tops of the houses in the old Town opposite to us. How long it had remained I cannot say, as we did not observe it till a few minutes before it cleared away. The sky then appeared bright for a short space, but the mist soon fell again like a curtain, thicker and lower than before. I do not remember that it was attended with dampness; and the whole perhaps was over in less than an hour.

We left Moffatt on the 9th of July, which happened to be the general Fast-day. We proceeded to Dumfries, which had been described as a Place of uncommon beauty; but herein we were disappointed. The Town is irregular and very closely built; almost all the Buildings of a deep red, ornamented with a different colour. The surrounding countryside was pleasant, and there was a public walk in the neighbourhood, with Water and high Trees, that was very inviting. We visited the Church Yard as usual; and found it uncommonly crowded with Tomb-Stones (even for Scotland, where monumental inscriptions are far more general than with us); and, for the first time in that country, found an inscription which breathed the spirit of genuine piety. I wish I had transcribed it. It was long, and part of it in good verse, and described a good and amiable woman living and dying in the spirit of the Gospel. The inscriptions in Scotland seldom give more than dates and names, and no holy Text "teaches the rustic moralist to die"; insomuch that they might all have been Pagans, for any reference that is made to the doctrines of the Gospel.

The only churchyard in Dumfries in 1807 was St Michael's, which is still full of large red sandstone memorials. Mrs Thompson's quotation is from Thomas Gray, in whose Country Churchyard even the humbler villagers had a text on their tombstones. Robert Burns' grave was in St Michael's churchyard, and may have been shown to visitors in 1807, though his mausoleum was not erected until 1815.[12]

Moffat Mineral Well, by David Allan (1795)
and as seen today

In our journey through the Borders we saw little variety. The lands appeared barren. Peat seemed the principal produce, large stacks of which were seen drying or preserving in the sun, like tiers of Bricks in a Brick yard. A large range of hills, standing East and West, was covered with Sheep, and it was amusing to see a shepherd and his dog bringing up hundreds at a time. The distance was too great for us to distinguish more than that the dog appeared to be sent to the skirts of the flock, which he drove before him without leaving a single straggler; and the Shepherd waited at perhaps a quarter of a mile distance, to guide them to another spot.

James Hogg the 'Ettrick Shepherd', who was coming into print about 1807, wrote this:- "Without the shepherd's dog, the whole of the open mountainous land in Scotland would not be worth a sixpence. It would require more hands to manage a stock [sic] of sheep, gather them from the hills, force them into houses and folds, and drive them to markets, than the profits of the whole stock were capable of maintaining."[13]

On the 10th of July we proceeded within sight of Solway Frith [sic], thro Annan, Gretna and Long Town, to Carlisle, where we spent two or three days very agreeably.

The Queensberry Arms in Annan was offered for sale in 1801, and described as the 'principal inn' in that town. The facilities advertised then give an idea of what the Thompsons may have looked for at any good Scottish inn. "An elegant dining room below and drawing room above stairs; four sitting rooms; twelve bed-rooms and three bed-closets; kitchen, scullery and pumpwell; stabling for 32 horses; a chaise house, granary, cow house and swine-hutts, with a good garden and large inn-yard .... commanding a beautiful prospect of the Solway frith [sic] from Carlisle to the Isle of Man"[14].

After Annan the travellers passed through Gretna, where one entered England by crossing the river Sark, and took the road on to Carlisle, which in 1807 went through Longtown.[15]

"The feast of Reason and the flow of Soul", constantly maintained at Carlisle Deanry [Deanery], took off the inclination for the inferior amusement of inspecting old buildings; and I know less of Carlisle than of most considerable places we passed through. The buildings appeared to bear the stamp of antiquity, and the City lively and cheerful, tho a good deal crowded.

The attraction at the Deanery was the Dean, Dr Isaac Milner. Perhaps best known as the man who guided William Wilberforce into evangelical Christianity, he was a family friend of the Thompsons, and, as President (head) of Queen's College, Cambridge, had guided their three sons through university. This portrait is by John Opie RA, Mrs Thompson's cousin by marriage.

Isaac Milner, Dean of Carlisle
by John Opie RA (1798)

"Diminutive compared with Scotland"
From 10 July 1807

Of the time afterwards spent at <u>the Lakes</u> I can give but little account, having kept no memorandums. Both the Lakes and Hills in Westmoreland, and indeed the whole scenery, are on so diminutive a scale, when compared with what we had seen in Scotland, that they appeared to great disadvantage. We thought Lancaster a very fine city, but staid little in it on account of the Assizes being held there at the time. The small village of Heysham on the Sea-coast had some curious remains of other times. It appeared as tho a Monastery of great extent had once stood there. Walls of amazing thickness were to be traced, and an antique gateway was still standing. But the most remarkable fragment of antiquity was a sort of rude stone Coffins, cut in one solid stone. I think there were five of them; not all of equal size, but one a little larger than the next, and so on to the smallest. No great attention to symmetry had been observed; and they seemed too small for full grown bodies. The tradition is that they have been formed before the Christian Era, but this I shd. think hardly probable.

> *The ancient building they saw at Heysham has been identified as St Patrick's Chapel, not a "monastery" but associated with the missionary disciples of St Columba. The rock-hewn graves nearby are still undated, but are possibly 10th century Viking.[1]*

I forgot to mention in its proper place that multitudes of people - men, women and children - were employed thro a large district in the Highlands in barking Trees. The Wood was of light growth, and the bark was peeled off in large pieces and stacked like bricks for baking. Whether the Trees would continue to thrive in that denuded State, or how such quantities of Bark are disposed of, I am not informed.

Wherever I have been in the northern parts of our Island, I have invariably found the wild flowers far superior in beauty to the same kinds growing in the South. The Hawthorn is uncommonly beautiful; and I thought the Woodbines, between Dumfries and Carlisle, surpassed any thing I had ever seen of the kind. There were likewise several different species of wild flowers which I had never observed before.

In our return out of Scotland we were desirous of seeing if there were any traces of a Barrier between the two countries, and desired our Chaise Driver to tell us when we came to the boundary. He stopped to tell us when we entered England, but there was no remains of a Wall, or visible separation.

I wished much to have seen the Cairn-Gorm, or Blue Mountain, one of the highest of the Grampian hills, which is said to be 4050 feet above the level of the Sea; but I believe we did not travel in that direction.

Cairn Gorm (4084 feet) is nearly fifty miles beyond Dunkeld, Mrs Thompson's furthest point north. Perhaps it symbolised, for her, the fact that there was still plenty of Scotland which she had not seen.

- o - o - o - o - o - o - o - o - o - o -

Scotch terms which were new to us

A Flat	- a floor.
A Turnpike	- a circular Stair case, on the outside of the house.
A Portioner	- a Yeoman, Renter of land.
Lawful Days	- Working days.
Mort Clothes	- Funeral Pall, etc.
Wull I?	- Shall I?
The hire's paid	- The Fare is paid.
Feued	- Rented; from feudal.
Manse	- Parsonage.
Haddie	- Haddocks. The fishwoman's cry.
Loch	- Lake.
Ben or Fell	- A Mountain.
The Precentor	- The Clerk in a church
To Demonstrate	- To preach. Not commonly used.
A Wynde	- An irregular narrow Street, or Alley.

POSTSCRIPT

Mrs Thompson's time in Scotland was a wonderful opportunity to see new scenes, and to have new experiences, in the company of her son John. I have letters which she wrote to him during the next two years, and they show how Scotland stayed in her mind. Certainly she never had such freedom again; and although there would be more journeys, they were mainly seeking relief from the illness which was overcoming her daughter and herself.

In December 1807 she borrowed Hugo Arnot's 'History of Edinburgh' from the Hull Library. "In many ways I find myself quite at home", she wrote to John. "Had I seen this book before I saw the City, I should have attended more to several places and things than I did." But she was shocked by Arnot's descriptions - perhaps a little out of date by then - of Scottish justice: of whippings without trial, and of youths in appalling prison conditions. "Were I to visit Edinburgh again", she goes on, "I would certainly contribute my mite of exertion towards the investigation of those evils."

A month later, work began on the piece of land at Cottingham, near Hull, where the Thompsons were to build a house called Cottingham Castle, and would do some farming. "We are going to visit our Policy", Mrs Thompson wrote to John, choosing the Scottish word for grounds round a large house; and went on, "We have bought 46 ewes and 52 lambs, though our flock would scarcely be discernible on a scottish range of hills". Visiting Ilkley in 1808, she went to Bolton Abbey: "It does not equal Melrose".

That year the Vicar of Cottingham died and Mrs Thompson was delighted when a Scot, Mr Deans from Aberdeen, was appointed. His sermons were "superior and well chosen". Mrs Deans was "lively and accomplished", and touched the local ladies so much by singing the Scots song 'Land o' the Leal' that Mrs Thompson copied it out in full for her son, closing her letter with its refrain: "Fare ye well, my ain John". In another letter of 1808 she asked John to suggest to "Walter Scott Esqre" that he write a factual poem about William Wallace - it would be "far more worthy of his Muse than idle fiction".

In 1809 John, already a graduate of Cambridge and on his way to becoming a barrister, spent about a year at Edinburgh University. The reason is not clear; but he attended the lectures of the famous philosopher Dugald Stewart, and enrolled in some medical classes. He wrote to his father from "Liddle's Lodgings" in South Hanover Street, Edinburgh, where he and his mother had stayed in 1807. She wrote to him there, in January 1809: "I am exceedingly glad, and so is your Aunt, that you have got to Mrs Liddel's [sic], as we have no doubt but you will be comfortable there. I suppose you have the Room at the end which was so crowded with pictures, some of which we hope may help to amuse you. Pray remember me kindly to your Hostess".

Liddle's Lodgings,
South Hanover Street,
Edinburgh. 12th Feb. 1809

My dear Father,

I am informed by a letter from my Aunt that you are on the point of setting off for London. I should be happy to go with you to the House of Commons, & to make my way to the Gallery notwithstanding the power of Mr Clementson & of Mr Taylor. But the Lectures I mean those of Mr Stewart, are not finished, & he gave notice

Letter from John Thompson to his father from Liddle's Lodgings, 1809

Later that month, she wrote to John about a review of Elizabeth Hamilton's 'The Cottagers of Glenburnie', which had just been published. She thought that the book sounded "little more than a libel on our admired Highlanders; and your Aunt thought the same. ... The Caledonians are undoubtedly in some instances dirty, and perhaps in others they may be lazy ... But there was nothing in that little Inn at the foot of Ben Lomond but what was decent and moderately comfortable, even to us south Britons ... If people have no stockings, they have no occasion to knit. But they are employed in far more laborious ways; and we saw no signs" - as 'Glenburnie' suggested - "of brushing tables down with the fingers; chusing a dirty knife to cut the butter; and various other matters which that book mentions as characteristic of the Highlands. When a writer talks of bad, i.e. boggy, Turnpike roads in Scotland, it leads to a suspicion that he has never been far North. If I remember right, there are no Turnpikes at all; yet the roads are always sound, tho they may possibly in some places be rugged". Mrs Thompson adds that she had only read the review of 'Glenburnie' (which in fact is a sympathetic view of rural Scotland, by a Scot): but she stood ready to defend the country which had given her so much pleasure in 1807.

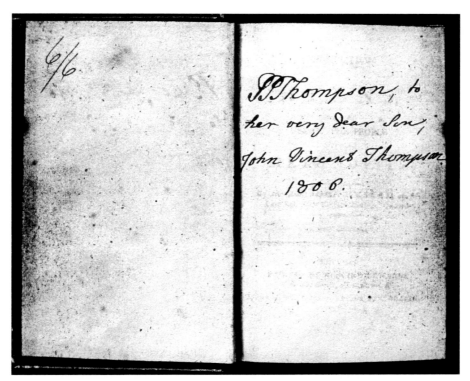

Mrs Thompson's signature, in a hymn book given to John

The letters give glimpses of the writer, at home in Yorkshire. Thus in December 1807, the month when she recommended Hugo Arnot to John, she apologised for some delay in writing to him. It was because of "My accustomed winter indisposition, increased by the epidemic cold sometimes called the Influenza; the shortening of daylight in Hull, with my increasing inability to do much by candle-light; together with my customary Christmas applications from the needy".

I will complete her family story quite briefly.

Her husband, Thomas Thompson, having entered Parliament in 1807, served there until 1818, speaking on proper wages for labourers; on the rival merits of gold coins or bank notes; on the treatment of the insane; on the price of corn; on the promotion of education in India; and on the morality of State lotteries. He began to keep a diary in 1814, when he reached the age of sixty, recording both past memories and ongoing events. He continued as a merchant and banker until after his wife's death. In 1828, aged seventy four, he went abroad for the first time in his life; died in France; and is buried in Paris.

Soon after his mother's Scottish tour the Thompsons' eldest son, Thomas, was invited by William Wilberforce to become Governor of Sierra Leone, the colony for freed slaves, at the early age of twenty five. He proved too liberal for the British Government; returned to the army; and was later a Radical MP. His long career in navy, army and politics is in the Dictionary of National Biography.

The youngest son, Charles, at Cambridge during the Scottish tour, won a Travelling Fellowship to visit Malta and Egypt in 1810-1811, from where he sent reports to Cambridge University, in Latin. While abroad he joined the Anglo-Sicilian Regiment as an officer; transferred to the 1st (Grenadier) Guards; and was killed in France in 1813. He had been a young man of enormous promise, wrote Isaac Milner, whom his mother had visited in Carlisle when returning from Scotland.

The middle son, John, was my great great grandfather. Having gone to Scotland with his mother, and done further study in Edinburgh, he was called to the English Bar in 1813. By then the British government was promoting education in India, and John nearly accepted a twelve-year professorship there, but withdrew to help his parents when his brother was killed, practising law in London instead. His wife was daughter of John Alderson, physician of Hull.

Philothea stayed at home. Carefully educated, and sharing her parents' religious beliefs, she still retained a lively mind. A tongue-in-cheek letter to John when she was seventeen describes her father's detailed instructions for their new house, and a young salesman's attempts to sell her jewellery while "Papa" looked on. That year Mrs Thompson wrote of her wish to keep Philothea "sheltered" for two or three years more, and of the need for a girl to feel love more than to "fall in love". "Take care of her", she wrote to John; "you will not have such another". Philothea had good friends, but remained single.

Meanwhile both mother and daughter had a 'malady of the lungs'. Over the years they visited the spas of Knaresborough, Ilkley, Hotwell and Bath. Both underwent the harsh remedies for consumption - bleeding, cupping, blistering and purging. In 1816 Philothea had an undisclosed surgical operation to help her breathing. Finally, in December 1822, mother and daughter travelled to Cornwall in search of warmer weather. Mrs Thompson died at Penzance, aged sixty nine. Philothea, for whom the Scottish diary was written, died in the same place three months later, aged thirty two.

DIED

At her lodgings at Penzance, where she had been to avoid the greater severity of the season at her usual residence in Yorkshire, Mrs. Thompson, wife of —————— Thompson, Esq.

Notice of Mrs Thompson's death in the 'West Briton' newspaper, 4 February 1823

Bibliography

'Argyll Forest Park' (Forestry Commission 1992)

Barclay, 'English Dictionary & Gazeteer' (London 1816)

Birrell J. F., 'An Edinburgh alphabet' (Mercat Press 1980)

Boyd J., 'Moffat, 17th to 20th century' (Moffat Museum 1987)

Burns R., 'Selected poems' (Penguin 1996)

Canongate Kirk, Edinburgh: guidebook 2005

Collier C. & Stewart L.A.,'Wooler & Glendale: a brief history' (Glendale Local History Society 1986)

Combe W., 'The tour of Doctor Prosody ... through Scotland' (London 1821)

Copeland J., 'Roads & their traffic 1750-1850' (David & Charles 1986)

'Cross Keys Hotel, Kelso: a short history' (pamphlet from hotel)

Curry I., 'Sense & sensitivity: Durham Cathedral & its architects'
(Durham Cathedral Lecture 1985)

Denholm J., 'The history of the city of Glasgow & suburbs' (Glasgow 1804)

Dictionary of National Biography (OUP 1885-1900 edition)

Donnachie I. L. & Butt J., 'The Wilsons of Wilsontown Ironworks 1779-1813'
(Explorations in Entrepreneurial History, 2nd Series, 1967)

Earl J., 'In search of a lost route' (in 'The Northumbrian', Spring 1994)

Eayrs G. (ed), 'Letters of John Wesley' (Hodder & Stoughton 1915)

Flaxington D., 'The history of Heysham' (Heysham Heritage Association 2001)

Forest W., 'The County of Lanark from actual survey' (map of 1816)

Fraser A., 'Mary Queen of Scots' (Weidenfeld & Nicholson 1969)

Galt J., 'Annals of the Parish' (Published 1821, J. M. Dent edition 1910)

Gifford G., McWilliam C. & Walker C., 'The buildings of Scotland: Edinburgh' (Penguin 1984)

Gittings R., 'John Keats' (Penguin reprint 2001)

Graham H.G., 'The social life of Scotland in the 18th century' (Adam & Charles Black 1906)

Hall Rev. J., 'Travels in Scotland by an unusual route' (London 1807)

Hamilton E., 'The cottagers of Glenburnie' (Edinburgh 1808)

'Heriot's Hospital' (pub. George Heriot's School, Edinburgh)

Hindley G., 'A history of roads' (Peter Davies, London 1971)

'History of St Andrew's Church, Kelso' (pamphlet from church)

Hogg J., 'The Shepherd's Calendar' (1829)

Hutchison J. D. & McFeat G., 'Douglasdale: history and traditions (Blackie & Co 1940)

'Illustrated road book of Scotland' (Automobile Association 1972)

Joyce M., 'Edinburgh: the golden age' (Longmans Green & Co. 1951)

Keay J. & J., 'Encyclopaedia of Scotland (Harper Collins 1994)

Landmark Trust pamphlet on Rosslyn Castle

Lee M., 'The heiresses of Buccleuch' (Tuckwell Press 1996)

'Melrose Abbey' (Historic Scotland 1999)

Mitchell A., 'Historic Kelso' (Kelso 1999)

Moffat A., 'The Borders: a history' (Deerpark Press 2002)

Pennant T., 'A tour in Scotland, 1769' (reprinted Birlinn Press 2000)

'Perthshire in Trust' (National Trust for Scotland)

Porson & White, 'Directory of Northumberland 1827-8' (pub. 1828)

Porteous A., 'The history of Crieff' (Oliphant, Anderson & Ferrier 1912)

Pyne W.H. & Gray C., 'Microcosm: a picturesque delineation of the arts, etc' (William Miller 1808)

Robinson A.R.B., 'The Counting House: Thomas Thompson of Hull (1754-1828) & his family' (Ebor Press 1992)

Scott Sir W., 'The lay of the last minstrel' (1805)

'The first Wearmouth Bridge' (Sunderland Local Studies Department)

Thompson P.P., manuscript letters 1795-1821, owned by the editor

Trainer J., 'Kelso Old & Sprouston Parish Church: a history' (Kelso Old Church 1992)

Wesley J., 'Letters of John Wesley' (8 vols., Epworth Press 1931)

Whyte I., 'Edinburgh and the Borders: landscape heritage' (David & Charles 1990)

Wordsworth D., 'Recollections of a tour made in Scotland' (Journal of 1803, first published 1874)

NOTES

Introduction

1 Eayrs G., 'Letters of Wesley'; letters addressed to Miss Phil Briggs, 1769-74
2 See references to John's aunt in my Postscript
3 Hindley G., 'A history of roads', p 61-7
4 Copeland J., 'Roads & their traffic', p 153
5 Pyne W.H., 'Microcosm', p 39

North to the Border

1 Curry I., 'Sense & sensitivity'
2 'The first Wearmouth Bridge'
3 Canon Peter Strange (Newcastle Cathedral): information supplied
4 Lord Ridley (Blagdon, Newcastle): information supplied
5 Earl J., 'In search of a lost route'
6 Adrian Officer (Whittingham, Northumberland): information supplied
7 Porson & White, 'Directory of Northumberland'
8 Alastair Lyell (Pallinsburn): information supplied

Chapel, Kirk and Abbey

1 Mary Balfour (Kelso): information supplied
2 Trainer J., 'Kelso Old & Sprouston Chruch'
3 Rev. James Crichton (Dalrymple): information supplied
4 'Cross Keys Hotel, Kelso'
5   'Melrose Abbey', & further information from Historic Scotland
6 Scott Sir W., 'The lay of the last minstrel', canto 2.1

The contrasts of Edinburgh

1 Thompson P.P., manuscript letters
2 Birrell J.F., 'An Edinburgh alphabet', p 245
3 Dr. David Rae, Edinburgh Botanic Garden: information supplied
4 Birrell J.F., 'An Edinburgh alphabet', p 34
5 Wesley J., 'Letters': letter of 29.9.1773
6 John Howard (Edinburgh): information supplied
7 Landmark Trust, pamphlet on Rosslyn Castle
8 Sandra Howat (Secretary to the Duke of Buccleuch): information supplied
9 Pennant T., 'A tour in Scotland', p 45
10 Lee M., 'The heiresses of Buccleugh', p 2
11 Joyce M., 'Edinburgh: the golden age', p 91
12 Birrell J.F., 'An Edinburgh alphabet', p 207
13 Birrell J.F., 'An Edinburgh alphabet', p 119
14 D.N.B.: Count von Rumford 1753-1814
15 Whyte I., 'Edinburgh and The Borders', p 195
16 D.N.B.: George Hill 1750-1819
17 Copeland J., 'Roads & their traffic', p 160
18 Rev. James Crichton: information supplied
19 Thompson P.P., manuscript letters

"By Lochs and Craggs"

1 'Illustrated road book of Scotland', p 209
2 ibid, p 162
3 Rev. James Crichton: information supplied
4 Pennant T., 'A tour in Scotland', p160
5 Wordsworth D., 'Recollections of a tour', 27.8.1803
6 Christopher Dingwall (Blairgowrie): information supplied
7 A. K. Bell Library, Perth: information supplied
8 Galt J., 'Annals of the Parish', p 31
9 Porteous A., 'History of Crieff', p 124; and information supplied by Nancy Johnston (Crieff)
10 Rev. James Crichton: information supplied
11 Hall J., 'Travels in Scotland', p 351
12 Galt J., 'Annals of the Parish', p 144
13 Nancy Johnston (Crieff): information supplied
14 ibid: from National Archives, Edinburgh, CH2/545/19
15 Canongate Kirk guidebook
16 Rev. James Crichton: information supplied
17 Burns R., 'Selected poems', p 86
18 Hall Rev. J., 'Travels in Scotland', p 255
19 Gillian Kelly (National Trust for Scotland, Dunkeld): information supplied
20 'Perthshire in Trust', p 17
21 Pennant T., 'A tour in Scotland', p57
22 'Perthshire in Trust', p 17
23 D.N.B.: James Macpherson 1736-1796
24 Dr. Brian Coppins, Edinburgh Botanic Garden: information supplied
25 Fraser A., 'Mary Queen of Scots', p 115
26 Barclay 'English dictionary & gazeteer', re Alloa

"Greatly delighted with Glasgow"

1 Pennant T., 'A tour in Scotland', p 154
2 Denholm J., 'The history of the city of Glasgow'
3 Guthrie Hutton (Glasgow): information supplied
4 Denholm J., 'The history ...', p 433
5 Alex Hall (Glasgow): information supplied
6 Denholm J., 'The history ...', p 140
7 Hall, Rev. J., 'Travels in Scotland', p 564
8 Keay J. & J., 'Encyclopaedia of Scotland', p 431-3

"An excursion into the Highlands"

1 National Glass Centre, Sunderland: information supplied
2 Dumbarton Library: information supplied
3 "Argyll Forest Park", p 30
4 The late Duke of Argyll; information supplied
5 Gittings R., 'John Keats', p 226

New industries and an old Saint

1   Rev. Alan Birss (Paisley): information supplied
2   Hall Rev. J., 'Travels in Scotland', p 573
3   Robinson A.R.B., 'The Counting House', p 72
4   Lorna Davidson (New Lanark Conservation): information supplied
5   Wordsworth D., 'Recollections of a Tour', 22.8.1803
6   Hamilton Library: information supplied
7   Donnachie I. & Butt J., 'The Wilsons of Wilsontown'
8   Hutchison J. D. and McFeat G., 'Douglasdale', p 156
9   Forrest W., map:'The County of Lanark', supplied by Lanark Library
10 John Murray (Moffat Museum): information supplied
11 Rev. James Crichton: information supplied
12 Dumfries & Galloway Library: information supplied
13 Hogg J., 'The Shepherd's Calendar'
14 Advertisement in 'Dumfries Weekly Journal', 20.1.1801, supplied by Dumfries & Galloway Libraries
15 'Illustrated road book of Scotland', entries for Gretna and Longtown

"Diminutive compared with Scotland"

1   Flaxington D., 'The history of Heysham', p 29

Postscript

All biographical details are from Robinson A. R. B., 'The Counting House'.

INDEX OF PLACES VISITED